The Reality

The Reality

*Successful change for people
and organisations*

BOB STOTT
WITH
GEORGE EDWARDS

Institute of Leadership & Management
1 Giltspur Street
London EC1A 9DD
United Kingdom

Tel: +44 (0)20 7294 8241
Fax: +44 (0)20 7294 2402
E-mail: info@i-l-m.com
Website: http://www.i-l-m.com

First published in Great Britain in 2004

ISBN: 1 902475 24 0

© ILM, 2004

British Library Cataloguing-in-Publication Data.

A catalogue record for this book is available from the British Library.

Book production by Chandos Publishing (Oxford) Limited (www.chandospublishing.com)
Typeset by Monolith (www.monolith.uk.com)
Printed in the UK by 4Edge Limited (www.4edge.co.uk)

Contents

Preface

Throughout the industrialised world rivers have for decades become choked with industrial toxins and other pollution. In this period all the wildlife which traditionally lived along their banks was displaced, some became almost extinct. But recently progress has been made in tackling this pollution, and many rivers are cleaner than they have been for almost 200 years. Their transformation has even heralded a comeback for otters, salmon and the kingfisher for the first time since the Industrial Revolution.

The kingfisher is especially important. This tiny turquoise bird is indigenous to most of the industrialised world – a nearly global species. It depends entirely on clean water, cannot be artificially introduced or released into an environment, but will return when the environment again meets its needs. Its reappearance is often the first sign that the waters have returned to health. This first sighting of a kingfisher along a river or canal bank means that a pollution crisis has been reversed. It is a sign that somewhere, in the boardrooms or the factories, possibly half a world away, information has been uncovered, its significance understood and the right decisions taken – and the world has indeed changed as a result.

About the authors

A former national chairman and corporate Fellow of the ILM, **Bob Stott** commenced his training as an engineer in 1962 with A. Reyrolle & Company, a famous switchgear manufacturers in his native North East of England. He remained with this evolving organisation for 23 years, progressing through a varied range of senior management and human resources roles as well as taking advantage of research secondments which were offered. This experience took him to work for Britain's Department of Trade and Industry, the Engineering Employers Federation and several universities and polytechnics. Since 1985 he has worked as a consultant with many different clients from the public, private and not-for-profit sectors in Britain and America, helping them to understand the processes that underpin lean manufacturing and corporate change. The research that culminated in the development of 'Secundi' was triggered by his involvement in a radical change programme for an American manufacturing organisation, and the realisation that 'conventional wisdom' regarding change was quite inadequate for the needs of organisations and their leaders in the twenty-first century.

See the author's website at:

http://www.secundi.com

Educated in New Zealand, Malta and the United Kingdom, **George Edwards** is a Fellow of ILM and of Britain's Royal Society for the Encouragement of Arts, Manufactures and Commerces. He graduated as a teacher from Oxford, England, and had a brief career schoolteaching in Britain and Zambia, before joining British Aerospace as an instructor in the Middle East. After rising to senior instructor, he subsequently worked for Saudi Arabian Airlines in Jeddah, and then as consultant to Kuwait National Petroleum and later Olivetti personal computers in Italy. In Italy he spent some years working in factory automation and control systems, before returning to the UK where he worked with the Engineering Industry Training Board. He has designed management qualifications for team leaders and trainers and accreditation processes for the Institute of Leadership and Management, and written over 20 books on management and training.

See the author's website at:

http://www.TheGeorgeEdwards.com

Introduction

Introducing the key characteristics of successful change leadership and the Secundi coefficient

> It's one of those heresies of the current century that you have to be an expert on something before there is any point in doing it. (Simon Barnes)

There must be a million quotations, aphorisms and general witticisms on the subject of change, and somewhere in cyberspace it is a fair bet that someone has compiled them. But this book is not going to add to them by more than a handful, because that is not its purpose. Having said which, the one above neatly sums up the essential proposition of the book so it seemed too good to omit. For we are all surrounded by change all of the time, none of us are experts, and we have no choice but to get on with it. With luck, and with practice, we will get better, but we don't really need or want to be experts. This book is for all the non-experts.

For in business as it is in life, there are options for how we relate to change. We can just accept the changes that time and the world impose on us, or we can seek to make the future better by taking some control of change, and so harness its power. The whole essence of leadership is managing change, and turning it from a directing force to directed power. It doesn't matter if you are talking about leading a company, a team of volunteers or simply leading yourself through your own life, the rules are the same.

A leader is someone who is followed. The leader may be the greatest living polar explorer, or your own heart may be doing the leading (and usually rushing off in the wrong direction). Where there is a leader, the term, the accolade, the distinction is because others follow. 'Leader' is not a description that you can award to yourself.

A leader will always take you to different, often new and unfamiliar, places. Sometimes the art is to take you safely to places that are inevitable, sometimes to take you to places different to those that mere fate would have taken you. Change always involves movement, travel, a departure point, a destination. You start where you are, but arrive at the place that the leader takes you, by the route that the leader chooses. Largely it is determination which affects how successful you are in reaching that point, how much pain or difficulty you encounter along the way or how swiftly you make the journey. Really, all leaders are change leaders. It is the successful leadership of change and the factors involved that form the basic theme of this book. The key is called the 'Secundi coefficient'.

The Secundi coefficient came out of more than a decade of work by Bob Stott in the North East of England. Bob Stott had been involved in a troubled change programme for a large American manufacturing organisation. He realised, as it floundered, that conventional organisational development tools and wisdom were failing to deliver successful change as the demands on organisations moved from the comfort zone of slow and incremental change, to rapid and radical threats. The essential failure was that of securing understanding in the organisation (the 'Secun' of Secundi). Without that clear and shared understanding of where the organisation actually was, no change process could succeed. However, with a clear and shared understanding, the organisation could successfully move into a renewed future ('delivering innovation', the 'di' of 'Secundi'). Convinced he was right, Bob began to address these issues, introducing a series of behavioural interventions to establish the conditions for change to succeed.

Bob was to discover that although the process largely succeeded, it was insecure. At the top of the organisation the culture had not been sufficiently changed, and inevitably the organisation began to drift, regressing into the habits that had originally made change so difficult to achieve. This convinced him that it was only when these habits were sufficiently firmly embedded that an organisation was equipped to face the near-continuous and radical change that is demanded of the 'survivor organisation'. Many years of interventions in changing organisations followed, the knowledge base growing as the strength of the process proved itself. By 1997, when Bob met George Edwards, the essential character of the coefficient was established, the terminology of Recognition, Reality, Reconciliation and Resolution was set. But it was only through several years of walking the boundaries around small Yorkshire towns and North East coasts that the process and the coefficient coalesced. What emerged was a quick, easy-to-use tool for measuring the current probability of successful change.

In this book therefore the authors explore these four important concepts in terms of their importance as the essential capabilities of the change leader which hold true in any situation. First, there is the ability to recognise the present, to see clearly where the individual, organisation or society is. As individuals, employees or citizens, it is not always clear where we are. We are so intimately involved in our own existence that, like examining a great painting too closely, we fail to see the totality. We only have a true view when as far as possible we have garnered not only the small details as we see them, but those that others see and point out to us. This stage in our change leadership is the establishment of Recognition, it is the secure ground from which we step off towards our destination.

From the achievement of Recognition we are able better to see the place we need to travel to. It may be a long journey or it may be a short step. To make the move, we must be confident of the direction. If we are unsure of where we are at present, we can never be certain that our first step is in the right direction. It is seldom true, as George Harrison famously suggested, 'If you don't know where you're going, any road will take you there'. For there is a difference between not knowing absolutely where life's journey will take you – largely true for us all – and not caring. We can all take decisions that will control life's destiny, but only if we care enough to try and find out the range of our possible destinations. The process of establishing the point to which we must proceed is the establishment of the Reality, and the Reality gives us our direction.

Between Recognition and Reality lies a gap. The gap may be wide, it may be deep, or steep, or appear uncrossable. We know that to succeed with the change that we have determined to undertake we need to set out the route, to plan the journey, to establish the tools and support that we will need. No one succeeds in change on their own. Even the most personal life changes, be they to do with health or finance, love or loss, depend on the feedback of others and on what our environment does in response to our actions. The route we plan, all the tools we gather, the help we identify, is known as the Reconciliation, and it is the job of the leader to determine it.

There is one final element of the equation that helps us to define the route to successful change. That is our Resolution. It is easy when one reaches the point of Reconciliation to decide it all seems too much, too far, too difficult. It is possible to lose heart at the immensity of the task, or to fail to achieve the goal through a lack of determination. The leader, the good change leader, will have the power to provide resolve, will draw on all the resources to maintain that resolve, and through all the difficulties and unexpected diversions will maintain that Resolution. Call it motivation, inspiration, determination, charisma. Some just call it 'leadership' in itself. In this book we call it Resolution.

The Secundi coefficient is thus the mathematical expression of the relationships between the four variables of change. The four values are:

- Recognition – the value assigned to clear understanding of the present situation;

- Reality – the value assigned to the clear understanding of the desired future position;

- Reconciliation – the value assigned to the clear understanding of how to move from Recognition to Reality;

- Resolution – the value assigned to the motivation that exists to achieve that reconciliation.

This mathematical expression is shown below:

$$\frac{\text{Recognition} + \text{Reality} + \text{Reconciliation}}{\text{Resolution}}$$

where the Reconciliation, Reality and Reconciliation are each values out of a maximum of 10, and Resolution is 30.

The theory behind the Secundi coefficient holds that these four factors are interrelated, and that they act not separately but cumulatively on the organisation or individual undergoing change. Further, Secundi shows that if a value can be put on each of the factors, the probability of successful change can be approximated as a mathematical value.

If we have very little idea of the truth of where we are, our Recognition is a very low value, and inevitably our Reality, where we must be as a result of change, is also low. Not knowing where we are or where we need to go means that inevitably our route, our Reconciliation, is uncertain, so also has a low value. It really does not matter how much determination we have, the value of our Resolution, our score is going to be low, our chances of success in the change process small.

The other end of the change spectrum is defined by high scores. After exploration, we should know almost exactly where we stand and hence achieve a high value for Recognition. Our Recognition starkly illuminates our Reality, and we can award a high score for Reality too. Given the clarity these two high scores signify, our Reconciliation, the path from Recognition to Reality, should be obvious. Knowing with security that we are in full control of these three factors we can be sure of our Resolution. Our chances of successful change are consequently high.

Between these two positions lie many possibilities, and this book is about how these four factors vary and the implications of their variation. The book will show how, through the 'Secundi' process, they give us the insight we need to effectively lead radical personal and organisational change, for it is radical change that is the true challenge of today. We have become used to incremental change, to adjusting the tiller slightly to alter our bearing as a gentle wind pushes us off course, but the world is no longer characterised by such comfortable incremental change – it is radical change that we increasingly encounter. Secundi gives us a tool for quickly analysing the radical change scenarios we face, and increasing our prospects of success or even survival.

Understanding ourselves or our organisations is the single most important factor in bringing about any required and desirable change. The only way we have of understanding our world is through truth. Truth is not always as simple and shining as we would like it to be. The constant presentation of 'truth' is what keeps most newspapers alive, and as any reader knows, studying the contents of differing newspapers illustrates differing 'truths'. Even when truth is sought earnestly, when presented it will be disputed. The Secundi coefficient forces us all to confront the paradox of differing truths, for the consequence of 'un-truth' is the certainty that change will fail.

The world is full of 'case studies' that help us to understand the importance of uncovering the unvarnished truth. One of the characteristics that differentiates the successful organisation from the static or dying one, the successful person from the less successful, is the ability to transfer paradigms. That is, to take the experience and lessons from their context of origin and, by holding them up against new and different scenarios, calculate the extent to which they still hold true. The all-encompassing example of modern times has been the Internet, leaving its trail of millionaires and paupers, grand corporate edifices and distress sales behind it, as the concepts that sold shoes, books and holidays are applied to insurance, legal services and pizzas. Where the paradigm transfers, there is success.

In this book we will draw from scenes in many lives that we can recognise either as individuals or as an aspect of the world in which we work. Just as one of the most common responses to a tale told is 'something just like that happened to me once!', so we can all see in others' stories something of ourselves and the challenges we face. With each tale, each case, example or metaphor that follows, we hope to uncover how it throws light on our own situation, illustrating one or more of the four 'Rs' we hold to be the key to successful change leadership. Sometimes we have changed the names of real persons, and in a few cases a fictionalised account is drawn from a real one to shield a person or organisation, but whatever the nature of each section, it examines honestly the thesis we hold of the four key success factors for leading change: Recognition, Reality, Reconciliation and Resolution.

Signs of change

The importance of small signs in establishing Recognition and reflections on the realities they suggest

Sometimes we don't notice that change has been happening all around us. Then one day we get a sign that could all too easily have been missed, and we have to quickly re-examine the world we thought we knew. This is what happened one day in a field in the North of England, but has happened in a similar way all over the world, in many contexts, and it happened just like this ...

The man had stopped at the point where the river fell noisily over the weir, his hands deep in his pockets, thinking. Some of his thoughts were probably of the work he had left on the computer at home, some on his own problems, but mostly he was thinking of nothing in particular. His dog snuffled at the edge of the river, and as he looked down the bank, considering the prospect of wet paws on car upholstery, a flash of blue appeared in his peripheral vision.

It took an instant to recognise the flash, half a second to raise his head and sight the object as it flew a few centimetres from the river's surface, vanishing maybe a second later. A kingfisher. He had never seen one here before. He walked on, small dog now at his side, anxious to complete the walk and gain the biscuit for jumping rapidly back into the car.

A kingfisher was hugely significant. It meant the river was cleaner than ever. It meant the environment was healthy. It brought the country again to the margins of his small town, a step back from the seemingly unstoppable march of the shopping malls, car parks and light industrial units. It restored his faith.

And he thought, 'Yes, I must see it again. If I can. If I can be at the right place, and at the right time. If the bird was not a mere traveller, maybe on a scouting visit, but never to return.' He began to play around in his head with the best way to do this. Tomorrow he would bring the binoculars, maybe the camera. He wondered if the local paper should know – after all they ran enough stories about local pollution and its consequences. First, though, he needed to see it again to be sure that it really was here to stay.

Then there was the effort involved. The mid-morning break was just a ritual, something he did whenever small dog made its feelings urgent and when he was not deep in a file. He would look down to his left, see small dog entreating him to a walk, and save the file. Together they would get out of the house for thirty minutes most mornings, sometimes again in the afternoons. But there was no planning to it, and now he was trying to plan, to bend his day to the sighting of the bird. It wouldn't work. On the other hand, it was unlikely that the kingfisher had a fixed schedule either, so maybe that didn't matter so much.

It really boiled down to the effort required, which in these days of flexible working and mixed work and family demands was not something he could promise himself. Things would intervene. Deadlines would rule. Some days, he knew, small dog would do without, because the man, unlike the singer, did not like walking in the rain.

In fact, if he was honest, the chances of seeing that kingfisher again were about as slim as the chances of him losing a stone in weight this year. It just wasn't his Reality. Still, it had been nice, and had made him think. He walked back up the hill to the car, small dog dripping and shaking at heel, and tried to get his mind back to the work waiting for him at home. Actually, there was also something about this business of the 'kingfisher moment' itself.

Because Recognition in itself always leads to questions. Sometimes the Recognition has been to the effect that we are not where we have always believed ourselves to be. It is good when we learn that we are in a better place, but when it is a worse place we have to react. We react initially by examining what this new knowledge means for us, and what we need to do in response. It is the Recognition of the present that brings us up to the challenge of change.

The Secundi coefficient calculations

The illustrative Secundi calculations in this book use the authors' own scores for Recognition, Reality and Reconciliation in the cases they refer to. In a true Secundi change process in an organisation the scores arrived at would be as a result of many contributions and agreed after debate.

The more mathematically inclined reader needs to know also that the top line of the calculation (Recognition, Reality and Reconciliation) comprises three scores, each on a scale of 1 to 10. These do not equate to either conventional or percentage fractions. In a Secundi coefficient calculation – as opposed to a point in the process leading to the calculation – the 'fourth R', 'Resolution', always has a value of 30.

'Resolution' under Secundi derives from two routes. The first is from 'resolve', or determination. The second is the analysis of and removal of doubt from a situation, which is what Secundi delivers. In the calculation of the coefficient, once the top line result is taken to be settled and true, as a result of this process seeing the situation clearly, 'Resolution' can only be full. The 'fourth R' therefore always has a value of 30.

To take an example that many will recognise, 'giving up smoking'. The would-be ex-smoker (not the person who is happy enough to continue) has no problem with Recognition and Reality. They will each be scored at 9 or 10. However, the problem is the score for Reconciliation, 'how to do it'. Until an acceptable and workable method has been devised, and this is consequently able to be scored at 9 or 10, there is no question of 'R4' even being awarded a value, as failure is almost certain. When, however, Reconciliation is finally possible, full Resolution will have been reached, so a full value of 30 is justified at that time. Things may change during the subsequent process, as many will admit, but at each point the

Secundi calculation produces a 'snapshot' of the current situation, and the likelihood of success if any weaknesses in the top line are not addressed. It is a tool from which it is always possible to determine a route forward, and improve the chances of success by addressing the issues uncovered.

3

The blind organisation

Never ignore the prophets of doom – they may
be the only prophets you have

In many companies there are, often tucked away in obscure positions, people who keep their eyes open and notice things that their colleagues 'miss'. They are the people Dr Meridith Belbin classified as 'Resource Investigators'. They tend to be extroverts in their daily lives, or at least in the lives that others see. They are enthusiasts, getting hooked on ideas and then sharing them, often controversially, with others. They develop unusual contacts and networks, convinced that even the most unlikely encounter feeds into the store of useful knowledge. They keep seeing opportunities, and will come up with a stream of initiatives that 'are really important' to their organisations. In order not to be overwhelmed, their colleagues keep dampening their enthusiasm down, and as a result the resource investigators can lose heart and become 'prophets of doom', causing even their most significant ideas to be brushed aside. Bill Chutman was a typical resource investigator.

In the dark, old-fashioned, metal-bashing Midlands of the country was a new industrial estate, just off the beltway that sneaked between the twin tower blocks, which in turn were built over the old gas storage tanks that once fed the heavy industry, direct descendent of the primitive metal works the first settlers had set up for their more basic needs. Now the business was all in services and technology, and on the glittering industrial estate was the new building housing Chambers Urostyle Limited, a remote metering company, which had raced from the small business start-up by the three original owners to a world-wide staff of 400 in less than a decade.

In the corridor the finance director and the product development manager were nearly at each other's throats again. The manager was a hard nosed ex-physicist and rugby player who had long escaped the dreamier corridors of his university position, forced out of academe through university cutbacks and the need to fund expensive education for his teenage children. Several career moves had brought him to Chambers Urostyle Limited. Bill still enjoyed an occasional visit to his old employer's science park, where he could, as he put it, 'enjoy conversations with intelligent life forms'. He didn't like the finance director because he judged him to be a fool.

Partly this was also because the financial director had never had what Bill felt was 'a real job'. He had gone straight from his chartered accountancy programme into work for a specialist caravan and trailer finance house before, through personal contacts, arriving at Chambers Urostyle soon after it began, with a salary more than adequate for his needs and the usual director's options. So he had stuck his feet firmly under a new desk, ordered some pictures for the walls and stayed put.

Now Bill was being told by someone he had been heard to refer to as a 'jumped up little abacus-rat' to 'get real'. As if he wasn't real. No one else in the damn company knew what was real, for pity's sake. They didn't keep their ears to the ground outside, didn't read the research, maintain the personal networks, do the blue skies thinking. They wouldn't see a trend if it was biting their arm off. They just got the boxes out of the door, that's what they did. And the finance director counted the boxes on his spreadsheets, added up the books and practised a fine line in meaningless platitudes, especially when he was feeling hungover or queasy about the month's numbers. Bill thought he must have a list of daily platitudes in his top drawer.

'Sam', said Bill (in that polite tone which means 'I think you are a fool but I'm not actually saying so'), 'will you just occasionally, for everyone's sake, stop using meaningless and occasionally offensive jargon? In the last couple of years you and your mates on the top floor have had us all being "world classed", we've had "total quality management", I still bear the scars of "Kaizen", those five wretched "Ss", some damn system called six sigma which to this day I cannot see as rocket science, and which I seem to recall cost us a fortune in consultants.'

He paused, but not for long enough to let his colleague into the conversation, which in reality had become a monologue and was in danger of slipping into a rant. 'Your problem is, you see, in common with most of the top floor, that you think you need all this claptrap to tell us how we can maintain our position. We don't', he poked a finger into the

FDs midriff, 'need' – another poke – 'to maintain' – poke – 'our position. We need', he feinted a poke, '*not*, that's N-O-T, to maintain our position. We need to M-O-V-E from our position, or we are going to D-I-E.' Bill paused. 'You see, you never think about the little signs. Remember when I came to the board four years ago when I'd just come back from that visit – what did you call it – "my jolly"? – to Ericsson? They'd got this research on a short-range radio link going on? Remember? I said it could mean drive-by metering. Did anyone believe me? Did they? *No*, of course not. But it only turned into Bluetooth, that's all.' Bill was rightly angry about this, and Sam knew that Chambers Urostyle had recently been struggling to catch up with some of the new players in the sector who had been faster to adopt the technology. Still, the top and bottom of it was that Bill hadn't even tried to make the case properly and so had let the company down. Heavens, he was having to deal with the fallout on the profit and loss sheet all the time.

Quite possibly in any other situation, or in any other company, Bill would have been thought to have overdone the lecture at this point, and spent the next few minutes filling up black plastic bags with the contents of his desk and returning his car keys. But the power balance in Chambers Urostyle was not like that, and so the finance director simply turned slightly pink and tried to laugh it off. Next, he knew, would be the stuff about 'recognition' and 'understanding the situation' and 'seeing what was really happening' and the usual blather.

So Sam chuckled in the way that only a better paid, more senior colleague can, which conveys precisely that he is overlooking some heinous behaviour by an underling, but doing it only because he was essentially a generous person. He routinely did the jocular forearm grab and the shoulder hug, and pronounced a pleasantry designed to get him away from Bill's finger and back up the stairs to his top-floor office and the slightly disturbing letter from their agents in Mexico. It had apparently been tough maintaining market share recently, and as everyone knew, market share was king.

It was, he reflected, a damn good thing for Bill that he was good at what he did, and that the directors knew their business inside out. He passed the picture of the kingfisher on the landing, not even seeing it, and turned right for his office. The door closed …

The Secundi coefficient at Chambers Urostyle

The company is clearly not good at seeing the whole picture. There may be other people who, like Bill Chutman, see a larger picture, but overall it is not sharing the vision. It is a fair bet that the head office doesn't really understand the concerns of its agents around the world. Recognition score of 5.

With impaired Recognition, it is difficult to see Reality. The directors, however, may see more from the 'helicopter view' than Bill realises, and certainly they have demonstrated the skills of building a company from small beginnings. However, the low Recognition makes it difficult to award a high Reality, because if you don't know where you are it is hard to see where to go. Reality score of 5 also.

Reconciliation is a consequence of Recognition and Reality. But if both current situation and desired end are unclear, the likelihood of getting the route to successful change right is very low indeed. It is impossible to award more than a Reconciliation score of 3.

Top line: Recognition 5 + Reality 5 + Reconciliation + 3 = 13

Their Secundi score is therefore 13 divided by Resolution (30), a coefficient of 0.43.

The maximum the company can achieve to be sure of successful change would be a coefficient of 1.0. To be reasonably confident for the future a coefficient value of 0.7–1.0 would be a good indicator. The chance of successful change in Chambers Urostyle – or in this case its survival – is very low at present.

4

The new generations

Do not expect social change or technological change to agree on which is driving! How our new generations are not going to play the old games we expect them to

One of the success stories of recent years has been the growth of 'interim management'. Originally intended to cover for managers who were ill, or to cover recruitment or maternity gaps, the role of the interim manager has been subtly changing. Now it is not uncommon for 'interims' to be recruited for specific projects, for defined short-term contracts. Such interims often command very substantial fees and are effectively 'leaders for hire', each with the mercenary's history of great 'interventions' they have led. The contracts tend to be short because the world is changing so fast. If a product or service is predicted to have a life of three years before major revision, a company needs to have it up and running quickly. Speed is a characteristic of modern change. When the Twin Towers were hit, British Airways reportedly had laid off 7,000 workers within seven days. When some Scottish farmed salmon was linked to carcinogens, Nutreco, one of the world's leading suppliers of fish food, was said to have seen its share value fall 20 per cent in just 24 hours.

So when, in 1964, a young Bob Dylan sang 'The times they are a-changin' he was simply repeating a universal truth. Even in the 1960s the message was not a new one. The changing times have presented a challenge to every generation since time began. Every generation has looked at the next and gently shaken its collective head in disbelief. The medical students at the University of Montpellier in the sixteenth century, according to the outraged townspeople, were just as impossible for their elders to understand as any modern students.

In the 1960s, however, the rate of change had still been relatively comfortable, and except to a few people or groups, not desperately threatening. The huge late twentieth-century collapses in employment had yet to come. It was possible, if erroneous, to still regard a job as 'for life'.

For the individual the rate of innovation was also comfortable rather than frightening. The birth control pill, often cited as the great invention of the 1960s, was in fact developed in the 1950s. Many commentators point out that its impact on the 1960s was confined to a relatively small section of society, and no one could see at the time how it would change the demographics of many countries, with its impact on pensions and on gross domestic products. The laser had been invented in 1960, but likewise no one then saw what would be its impact on the music industry some thirty years later, or the information storage revolution, making movies just another supermarket purchase by the early twenty-first century. In 1967 the world heard too of the first human heart transplant, but it was far, far away, in a country called South Africa. South Africa wasn't likely to matter much. The world – and life – moved on much as it always had. There was time for free love and flowers in the hair. Change was indeed accelerating, but quietly, largely unseen and apparently not yet threatening.

Forty years later everyone has a different relationship with their world. Life is no longer a gentle voyage on a rippled sea. The innovations of the late twentieth century have tumbled out into the world at a pace never seen before, and for many life is a choppy, storm-tossed crossing on an angry ocean. The new adults, the new workforce, have seen many technological and social developments go the complete cycle from discovery to oblivion. The personal pager and the home fax machine arrived, were adopted, became status symbols and then all but vanished. The portable telephone became the car-phone, became the mobile phone, became the web-phone, became the digital camera and the message centre. The one-hour photo processing shop, still a newcomer on the high street, began to give way itself as digital cameras became commonplace.

Partly because of this extraordinary acceleration of the rate of change, work for the later generations of the twentieth century has never even vaguely promised that 'job for life'. As old industries have closed and whole regions have been reshaped from industrial wastelands into 'sunrise' industrial estates and boom-bust new organisations, people have seen their parents and relatives employed and unemployed, transferred, retrained, relocated, downsized, delayered, head-counted and outsourced. One thing they know is that security is not a word to connect with employment. Consequently they do not return security to their employers. Take Cathy.

Cathy is a fairly normal girl for her age. Seventeen, and at a good local school, she is working hard for her high-school examinations and a college place. The exact nature of that college place is not definite yet, but one thing is certain, it will not be a decision based on job security or potential earnings. It will be something she chooses because it is going to be personally rewarding.

After all, her parents haven't exactly been advertisements for 'sensible' career decisions. Both 'baby boomers', they have together been through more career changes than she has had birthdays. Neither are now doing anything even remotely like the careers they had each gone to college to pursue.

She knows her Dad had spent four years learning to be a teacher. She knows that he had given that up after a few years as the job changed into something he had never expected. He had then had jobs with the military, and somehow managed to find himself in a job in a computer company. He had told her enough about industrial robots to surprise her. When she was a kid he had been a consultant, then something in engineering, and he had written books too.

Her Mum had been a teacher, something in the Indian health service, and a company director in Hong Kong. By the time Cathy was six her mother was high up in the British National Health Service, and just now she was starting another company. Most of her friends at school had similar parents. Her enlarged family was much the same, none of them apparently in the sort of 'sensible job' which she had heard of from her career advisers at school reciting career options as if they were Reality.

Cathy is looking at a world that will hold many futures, and already recognises that her first career might not last very long. So the decisions she has to make initially about her college course are going to be made for love, not money or security, and she will look to her own abilities and the experience she gains to carry her forward. She is comfortable with change, because she has lived with it. But she does need to manipulate change to her advantage, plan for the next five years, make the right decisions, evaluate the best moves. She needs a recipe for successful change. She has drawn up a plan for herself.

It begins with 'Where am I now?' and goes on to 'Where do I want to be?' and 'How do I get there?' Underpinning all the facts and possibilities, all the plans and back-up strategies, is a steely determination that she is not going to be messed about by life – from here on, she expects to control the changes that she encounters. Her plan does not include anywhere the concept of loyalty to an employer in exchange for long-term security. This is generation M, and it frightens organisations. It should frighten governments, for it can destroy their strategies in less than a decade.

Cathy's Secundi coefficient

Cathy is someone who has clearly been keeping her eyes wide open. Unlike more sheltered generations, life's events have been very apparent to her, and she has seen in her classmates and family many paradigms, both for success and failure. She is quite sure what the future holds for her, although she doesn't look too far ahead. She should be able to give herself a Recognition score of 8.

She has two favoured futures for the period between now and after graduation and has researched both options thoroughly on the Internet, through visits to colleges and copious reading of prospectuses. She sees her reality quite clearly, although she is well aware things can get in the way, and because of the potential for 'things to go wrong', her Reality score is about 7.

Like her Reality, Cathy has more than one Reconciliation open to her. However, she is fairly sure of at least the starting point of her path forward and of the main milestones. She would probably award herself a Reconciliation score of 7.5.

Top line: Recognition 8 + Reality 7 + Reconciliation + 7.5 = 22.5

Dividing by Resolution (30) produces a coefficient of 0.75, in line with her expectations. Her shortfall coefficient of 0.25 reflects what is yet to be understood, learnt and experienced, and which she will treat as a spur to success.

Cathy may have opted for a conventional college course herself, but many of her classmates will not be going on to college. For in the United Kingdom a change was introduced by the Labour government in the early years of the twenty-first century.

IT has made it possible for 'generation M' to have circles of close friends all around the world. Cathy and her friends may have mainly used instant messaging services to chat during homework, but the important thing is that they were doing their homework while on the Internet. Through it they have circles of acquaintance around the world, and these acquaintances speak – or write – English. They go to McDonald's, drink Pepsi, use Nokia phones, shop for clothes at Gap. Later, their friends will also go on to college and study in university departments in India or Beijing, but in English. To generation M there is already one global culture.

Generation M is also the most mobile the western world has ever seen. They have seen their own countries shrunk by air travel or high-speed rail, they were taken as babies for weekends in Cairo or New York, and later for vacations in Sri Lanka and the Caribbean. As teenagers they have enjoyed partying on Mediterranean islands or in Prague. Only money and time has been the barrier, and in an increasingly affluent West with falling transport costs and flexible working lives, even these barriers have been lowering.

Knowledge too is different for generation M. This is the Google generation. For them knowledge is just something you have delivered to your screen, not something that takes time to acquire – certainly not something that needs to be obtained slowly and at great cost. When they need some information about the basic tenets of Kaballah or the components of a flashlight battery, they can have it by broadband in three clicks. They use the information for just as long as it is useful to them, and dispose of it, secure in the knowledge that they can always click it back should they need it again.

It was into this environment and this most self-assured of generations that the Labour government launched its new policy for 'Higher Education' in the United Kingdom. The United Kingdom had long been proud of its policy of 'free' higher education, under which students were not charged for their tuition at college, although increasingly they had to meet their living costs through loans and working. The government had some years earlier adopted a target of persuading a full 50 per cent of all school leavers into degree-level education. They had expanded the availability of college places rapidly to meet this objective, thereby bringing about a steadily falling value of a degree to young graduates entering the workforce. This simple supply and demand effect, already apparent in 2000, was met by the response that any opposition to the policy was fuelled by a political attempt to deny youngsters the higher education they were entitled to.

In 2003 the government announced that generation M was to be the first generation to be required to pay towards their higher education tuition, and they introduced a law requiring this generation of students to pay so-called 'top-up fees'. This was, they said, the only reconciliation possible in a situation where underfunded universities were having to admit ever more students. There were many and manifest problems in this sudden policy change, but they were met by a process of rationalisation. The government eventually persuaded a hostile House of Commons – including many of their own members of parliament – to accept the reconciliation plan based on the Reality as the government wanted them to see it.

The country argued over what the truth was in the press, in the newspapers, on the radio and on television.

The government surely knows that generation M does not regard knowledge as expensive to obtain. It was already well known that the generation is intensely consumerist, and so if they are asked to pay for education, they will act like consumers. The government must also have known that the generation is the most mobile in history, and they have the pick of the world's universities to choose from, many still 'free'. For many decades successive British governments had been proud of being the home of the world's most widely used language for higher education and commerce, and so the government knew that there were English-speaking colleges all around the world, many of which did not intend to charge fees.

However, the government still managed to convince themselves that generation M would gladly spend three years accumulating large education debts in the pursuit of knowledge that might be of no value to their first employer, with whom in any case they only expect to remain for a couple of years before changing careers.

They also managed to rationalise away the impact on the future UK economy of a generation in debt, at the very time of their lives when they would also be increasingly desperately urged to save for personal pension provision. Having by rationalisation disposed of the Recognition and changed the Reality, with huge Resolution the fees policy was forced through the UK parliament.

Even while the fees law was being debated in Parliament, a British household survey showed that the value of a degree had fallen by up to 20 per cent in a decade, the first decade in which the 50 per cent target was being actively pursued by government. Before the law came into effect, a hurried change in the recently passed personal bankruptcy laws had to be made to prevent a large number of students making themselves bankrupt to avoid repaying their student debts. Shortly after the law was passed, a report by PA Consulting showed that UK universities themselves expected that, as a result of tuition fees, a significant number of newer universities would be forced to close. The report also showed that the value of a degree to employers continued to fall. Only weeks before the admission processes for the last generation of 'free' higher education students began, a change was hastily rushed through Parliament to avoid a huge number of students overwhelming universities ahead of the introduction of the fees.

Reconciliation not based on full Recognition and Reality produced through rationalisation produce false Reconciliation. When this is combined with a huge Resolution, it can have consequences that produce the worst possible outcomes.

Secundi coefficient for the introduction of tuition fees

The British government had a difficult task. In looking at higher education, it saw clearly the pressures the universities were under, having created many of them. It also looked to the future of employment, and recognised that in a competitive global environment, higher skills in the whole workforce are necessary. To balance this, however, it conflated higher skills with both higher education and higher qualifications. It also seemed to overlook some major changes in generational attitudes, demographic forecasting and the impact of technology on learning delivery.

It is useful in Secundi often to 'triangulate' views. There were a huge number who argued viscerally against the policy, and those who argued equally fiercely for it. These views are largely balanced out, and with the equal weight of many more thoughtful contributors on each side, a Recognition score of 5 enables the coefficient to be calculated. This in turn gives an opportunity for later re-examining the top-line scores, should either a very high or very low coefficient appear, which would be an unlikely outcome. A Recognition score of 5 seems to be a fair reflection of this situation.

It is by no means clear that the government addressed Reality without the blinkers of political philosophy. Even after the figures began to move against their main argument, they stuck to their insistence that the 'graduate premium from employment', the means by which student loans were to be repaid without pain, was not in decline. They had themselves already launched a number of initiatives in response to a national vocational skills shortage, mainly for non-graduate jobs, the real shortage area. Their Reality seemed to encompass assumptions that were untested. A score of 5 again reflects this confusion.

The reconciliation chosen was a 'new Labour, third way' solution. The government wished to 'embrace the market', although higher education in Britain could scarcely be described as a free market, riddled as it is with subsidies and inconsistencies. It also wanted to find a policy that would not require further government spending leading to raised taxes, never likely to be popular. In this dilemma it produced a reconciliation that was unlikely to fully solve the funding problem, yet would meet with huge and sustained opposition. It was likely, and widely predicted, that it would introduce a range of unforeseen consequences with potential to cause serious problems for years in many sectors of the economy. A Reconciliation score of 3.5 reflects the strategy.

Top line: Recognition 5 + Reality 5 + Reconciliation + 3.5 = 13.5

The Secundi coefficient for the first years of student top-up fees is therefore 13.5 divided by 30, a value of 0.45. Major problems seem to lie ahead, and changes will have to be made.

5

Creating common focus

How it is necessary to ensure the whole organisation shares Recognition, and a success story from Japan

The past is a great source of inspiration to us all. Perhaps because we are all raised with the axiom that 'history repeats itself' we feel we can, by studying the past, predict or control the future, turn again and again to the success tales of the past. This grates with the Reality of change. Very little of the world a young Bob Dylan saw around him in the 1960s remains. As L.P. Hartley put it, looking in the other direction, 'The past is a foreign country; they do things differently there', raising the puzzle of why we feel we can learn from it how to manage our present and future. But we do turn to the past for lessons, and some of these do withstand the journey from the past. One such lesson was being enacted in the final years of the twentieth century in one of the world's major manufacturing companies.

In 1912, Masujiro Hashimoto had joined with three partners to launch the Kwaishinsha Motor Car Company in Japan. Like FIAT (Fabbrica Italiana di Automobili Torino – 'The Italian Motor Factory in Turin') the company brand name was made of the initials of its founders, producing

DAT in English letters. The DAT brand name survived the merger with Jidosha Seizo in 1926, eventually emerging as DATson ('son of DAT') and then Datsun in the final reorganisation that produced in 1934 the Nissan Motor Company. Soon after this Nissan exported its first vehicles, and barring an interruption caused by the Second World War, steadily grew to a global brand. By the late twentieth century Nissan had been especially successful in North America, where it was known for small, efficient and well-made cars, tough pickup trucks, and a widely admired sports coupé, the 240Z and its successors. Nissan was a success, it was profitable, and four of the worlds ten favourite cars came out of its factories.

Throughout the 1990s the company acted like any big, secure, Japanese company of the time. It concentrated on protecting its existing market share, scarcely noticing as the decade went on that eventually only four of its 43 car models actually made a profit for the company. Its reputation for engineering and productivity led it to assume that the market would always choose such inner values in preference to the stylish, innovative cars its competitors were now producing. In America and other sophisticated markets the age-old battle with Toyota over both the sports car and the pickup markets became keener, but instead of a constant reinvestment in new products, Nissan followed the traditional practice – known as 'keiretsu' – of investing in other companies and in real estate. This common Japanese custom was believed to ensure the loyalty and support of the members of the value chain it created. By 1999, Nissan had tied up over $4 billion in this type of investment, $4 billion which was therefore not working for the company in terms of investment in new models and production systems.

This situation might have lead to a steady decline, or even been sustainable in the medium term, had there not been a financial crisis in the region, eventually forcing the devaluation of the Japanese yen by 10 per cent against the US dollar. This made the company's finances very weak, and in February 1999 two American credit rating agencies announced that if Nissan could not get some financial support, possibly from another car maker, it would downgrade Nissan shares from 'investment grade' to 'junk'. Under this pressure from the markets, in particular the North American market, it didn't take long for the Nissan board to belatedly understand that it had been ignoring the signs, rationalising its way out of taking the steps that it had to take and endangering the whole edifice. As in many organisations, systems were in place which in themselves helped to ensure the organisation could continue to deceive itself. Despite culture, opposition and the strength of Japanese industrial tradition, in March of that year a partner was found in France's Renault. Renault took a stake of 36.8 per cent in Nissan, freeing $5.4 billion for Nissan, and its credit rating was saved. Part of the deal was that Carlos Ghosn of Renault would take over the role of chief operating officer of Nissan.

Carlos Ghosn came out of the often tough world of leading global organisations. He had been with Michelin's Brazilian subsidiary in the era of runaway inflation in that country. Later, as head of Michelin's North American operation, he dealt with the complexities of their merger with Uniroyal

Goodrich, while at the same time steering the organisation through a major recession. Joining Renault as an executive vice president, he led the turnaround that Renault desperately needed after the failure of its attempted merger with Volvo. At Renault he earned the nickname 'le cost cutter', but his obsession with costs did greatly increase the automobile maker's margins. Now, with the move to Nissan, he had held key positions on four continents, and with five spoken languages, was considered a global-ranking organisational leader. He was to take just 12 months to make Nissan profitable again.

Legendarily, Ghosn was the first ever chief operating officer of Nissan to actually meet everyone in the company. The results of his consultations at all levels led to him finding the key to this turnaround, the use of cross functional teams or CFTs. These were able to overcome many of the cultural blocks to rapid progress that would otherwise have foiled the plan. He knew that these teams would be an essential tool for getting line managers to ask hard questions, challenge conventional thinking, see clearly and devise ways of improving their own activities.

In Nissan, as in many Japanese companies, there had been a tendency for departments to regard their own activities as proper and efficient, but to see other departments as weak and holding back progress. This was reinforced by the long-established culture of deference to the long service of other workers, and a dislike of open disagreement emerging in meetings, causing decisions to be delayed while consensus was reached informally over a long run-up period. Ghosn started immediately to create what he called 'transparency', based on his belief that an organisation can only be effective if everyone believes the same and that what their leaders say and what they do are the same thing.

By November of 1999 the teams were beginning to deliver. Not only were changes in employment terms, in working practices and decision-making improving, but the organisation itself began a restructuring with the disposal and closure of five factories and the loss of 14 per cent of its workforce. This was a very obvious rejection of the national culture of lifelong employment. When senior heads began to roll too, the media and industry analysts created a storm of objection. But inside Nissan changes were having a real impact.

The restructuring had included a focus on CFTs which each serviced one product line. As a result workers were beginning to see the entire business better, and to focus on customer satisfaction and on the success that their own contribution created for the total business rather than 'performance targets' in isolation. Soon Ghosn also took Nissan away from its culture of 'keiretsu' investment, freeing massive funds for debt reduction and thence for new product investment. This investment increased as Nissan drove down the cost of its purchases from suppliers, creating a virtuous financial circle. It became possible to create a performance-based reward system, a huge departure from normal Japanese practice, encouraging complete worker buy-in to the change process despite its pain. Promotion on merit replaced time-serving, and younger managers began to appear throughout the business.

By March 2002, one year ahead of schedule, the Nissan recovery plan was completed.

In fact this was a classic Recognition, Reality, Reconciliation, Resolution change process. Ghosn saw from his early interviews and his 'walking the company' that there was a problem of Recognition. The nature of the company had militated against all workers sharing a clear view of their situation. For example, the 1990s focus on market share had obstructed a clear view of what the competitors were actually doing, as an achieved market share was taken to mean that all was well. This enabled the rationalisation of threats from competitors and the changing needs and desires of consumers to the point where they vanished.

The internal communications, together with the company culture, also prevented important messages from being accurately received. So within every 'compartment', the view was fine. There was no sense of crisis, no threat of bankruptcy. The Japanese culture had always bailed out failing industries. But at about the same time as Ghosn arrived in Japan, a huge shock hit the company and the country as a whole – a major finance house collapsed and was not bailed out by the government. Bankruptcy could happen to Nissan too – the impossible was now possible.

The creation of CFTs enabled all workers to share a clear vision of where the company was. Changes to the internal culture, which on his appointment Ghosn had agreed to take into account, made it possible to quickly decide where the company had to go. The members of the first teams were often mid-level managers who had previously rarely seen beyond their own functional responsibilities, and this increased vision through the CFTs had a remarkable impact. They saw that their isolated measurements of success were meaningless without a clear idea of how these related to the achievement of the company as a whole. With this increased understanding, they became more engaged in the Ghosn change process and aware of their own responsibility for helping to turn Nissan around. Out of this had come the Nissan recovery plan, setting out the Reconciliation actions needed (including the highly contentious closure and redundancy elements) and creating Resolution throughout the whole workforce.

A view of the Nissan recovery, using the Secundi coefficient

One of Carlos Ghosn's cardinal rules was transparency, his belief that an organisation can only be effective if everyone believes the same and that what their leaders say and what they do are the same thing. This can only be achieved if everybody shares the truth of their situation and creates Recognition. Also helping to create recognition were his strategies of 'walking' the organisation, empowering the teams and appointing on talent. Together this created a very high score for Recognition in Nissan, certainly 9.

The reality at Nissan became apparent when the 1990s obsession with market share was stripped away and departments began to see how their competitors were moving ahead. The fact was that by the end of the 1990s the company had only four profitable models out of the 43 they made. It had also been brought up sharply by the previously unheard of possibility of bankruptcy and by the threat to their investment status. It was clear that the Reality required them to change, and change in line with global best practice. There really was no choice. There had been a caveat written into the Ghosn contract, however, and this was to avoid major clashes with the culture, especially job security and appointment on seniority. This does suggest that at the time Ghosn arrived, there was still negotiation as to the nature of Reality, and this might have remained around for the early months – certainly the Japanese media suggested it was still an issue. A score of 8 for Reality.

The Reconciliation Carlos Ghosn chose was an enabling one, requiring the cross-functional teams to develop the way forward and empowering them. As such it was not a single, clearly mapped route, but the mechanism of development and constant short steps to overall reconciliation. There was a risk to this strategy, but there was also huge determination, driven not only by Ghosn himself but by the starkness of the new Reality. We need to remember that Ghosn had experience of cross-functional teams already, and this lessened the risks that might otherwise have been associated with handing them such authority. Given that the risks were tightly controlled, the process monitored and the leader experienced, award 8.

Top line: Recognition 9 + Reality 8 + Reconciliation 8 = 25.

The Secundi coefficient for the early stages of the Nissan recovery programme was therefore 25 divided by 30, a value of 0.83. Major problems were unlikely, and the chances of success were twice the chances of failure.

6

Rationalisation

The dangers of 'rationalisation' and its use to protect the organisation from engaging in the change processes it needs to undergo

One of the features that often seems to characterise corporate and personal crisis is rationalisation. It was a feature of Nissan throughout the 1990s and was confronted only when Ghosn tore it away. Rationalisation is the consequence of fear, in that it represents one acceptable reason for not doing anything about any threats. As such it is a denial of Reality and can have disastrous consequences for individuals and organisations.

When in full flow, it actually fortifies itself, creating systems and processes to protect the rationalisation of problems rather than solving them. It is like a cancer in its outcome. It is in effect like standing still in the middle of the highway, and right up to the moment the inevitable happens saying, 'Well, I've never been knocked down before'. Let's consider the case of Markington Systems Limited.

Markington was a successful small business. It had around a thousand regular customers for its systems and enjoyed a degree of stability. The head office team had been in place for many years, and the systems and processes for delivering to customers flowed well. Each year saw a small profit, and with due care each year yielded a bonus for the staff.

Because of the nature of the product, the only competitor was GHDW, a company formed when, earlier in Markington's history, an attempt had been made to demerge a main Markington product line into a separate business. Over the years the resulting two organisations had been through degrees of cooperation and hostility, usually at the discretion of their respective chief operating officers. The market tended to see-saw between the two providers, often on the whim of an individual in the purchasing department or the personal preferences of the customer's chief executives. The products were remarkably similar, so such switching was annoying to both Markington and GHDW as it underlined the fact that neither had much to offer that their competitor couldn't do just as well.

In the mid-1990s a new director, Bill Williams, arrived at Markington. He had come from a different background, a far more customer-focused organisation, and looked closely at the situation in his first few months. What he saw was so blindingly obvious that to confirm it he spent almost six months going around Markington customers, ex-customers, GHDW customers and companies who were customers of neither. Then he addressed the management team with a proposal.

Both Markington and GHDW were essentially selling the same products in the same ways to the same limited number of buyers. There was almost no potential to grow the market, and the best that could be hoped was that they could sell more of the same to this existing customer pool.

But what Williams had discovered was that all the existing customers also had needs for services that they could buy neither from Markington nor GHDW. The reason they gave was always the same: that the elements they wanted were only available as part of the standard Markington and GHDW packages. In fact, to the customers, the part they wanted most, and the most potentially valuable to them as something they could in turn sell to their customers, almost always came with extras and complexities they didn't need. Certainly they would continue to buy the standard offerings, but again and again said that they would not increase their purchases because they couldn't themselves expand their customer base for the products incorporating the unwanted features.

Williams's question to the management team was stark. Why not sell cut-down products that each only contained the parts the customers wanted to buy? This could expand the business Markington did with each existing customer, but also attract in customers who would buy this new product but were not buying the present formulation from either Markington or GHDW.

The sense of shock was palpable. Markington had been around for over 40 years and the products had always been acceptable. It was not as if they hadn't evolved in that time. It wasn't as if anyone had ever asked for the formulation Williams suggested. Anyway, they were retaining market share and there would always be some customers who switched. They tended to come back one day. And the Markington business was basically sound, growing at about its historic rate. No one had suggested it was in danger. As one manager said, 'If it isn't broken, don't fix it.'

But Williams had been in tougher spots. At his previous company he had experienced the difficulties of launching a new product despite the initial opposition of the management team, and succeeded. He again set about winning hearts and minds at Markington. He retold pointed anecdotes as he returned from meetings with potential new customers and with former, profitable customers. He showed that many of the difficulties the customer service team dealt with, and a lot of the missed sales the sales force reported, could be analysed in terms of the product formulation that he proposed. He pointed out how it would add a second, less cyclical business stream and so improve cash flow over the year. And eventually he won the day, and eventually the new Williams product was born.

Williams took total control of the new product for the first year. The truth was that he had to because it had required systems and processes that history had not equipped Markington with. Also, he was still the only person who had travelled from Recognition through to Reconciliation. But as he grew the product, the results were spectacular. Within a year nearly one hundred completely new customers emerged, interested only in the new product. Some went on later to buy other more traditional Markington product packages, and importantly some ceased to buy the GHDW product they had been using for years and switched to Markington.

In the second year the Williams product grew faster than any product in Markington's history – at times it was the only growth Markington saw. Gradually the Markington team was won over, and as the whole company finally saw the Reality and the Reconciliation was correct, Resolution rocketed. The product was a winner.

At around the same time, in the board room a major change was being planned. The directors of GHDW had finally agreed to discuss a merger with Markington, something that alternate boards of the two companies had toyed with for a decade or more. The truth was that these were two very similar companies, and as a result each was spending much of their time defending market share in a fixed market. GHDW had taken note of the Williams product and noted the progress Markington was now making in its increasing visibility and growing reputation for innovative thinking. There was an inescapable logic to a merger, which after a decent interval duly took place

As a result, products were shuffled, systems rationalised, staff moved and replaced. When the shuffling had ceased, it was the former GHDW managers who emerged in control of the product range. They looked at the Williams product, and knowing it had done so much for Markington's recent development and its grip on the market and that it was a threat to their own 'successor products', they decided to kill it off by rationalising it out of the product line-up. It was, after all, not the way the new organisation did things.

After all, GHDW had been around for a long time before the merger, and their way of doing things and their systems and product lines had always been acceptable to the customers before. It was not as if their products hadn't evolved in that time. It wasn't as if anyone had ever asked them for such a strange product formulation as the 'Williams' product. Anyway, together the merged companies had almost total market domination. They could now insist that 'Williams customers' went back to the old products. There would always be some customers who switched to one of the very few remaining competitors. The business was basically sound, growing at about the predicted rate. As a manager said, 'If it isn't broken, don't fix it.' Williams himself was promoted sideways.

But then former Markington customers and the former GHDW sales team started talking to their former Markington counterparts and to the customers they had each inherited, and a large slice of the market began inconveniently to ask where the Williams product had gone. Customers were blunt with the sales team: they wanted to buy the Williams product or they would go elsewhere. It emerged, in a series of plain-talking encounters, that the systems the newly merged organisation were imposing were not nearly as popular with customers as they had always thought. And at about the same time, a change in the industry regulations meant that it was possible, just possible, that real growth might be delivered through the variations the Williams product had made possible.

So it was, finally, that, re-shaped slightly and with a new name to placate the former GHDW team that had opposed it so strongly, the Williams product re-emerged. But almost two years had passed by. A huge effort would be needed to reclaim former users, to retrain the sales force in the new features of the product, and a huge market advantage had for two whole years been deliberately ignored. Through-out, rationalisation had been used to counter the truth that had been revealed when Williams first began to apply the principles of Recognition, Reality, Reconciliation and Resolution, to produce the change Markington and its successor had desperately needed to undergo.

7

The cost of 'progress'

*The risk of letting technology drive change,
and how the cost of retaining knowledge is
less than the price of losing it*

Strangely, at the end of the day, it was really the voice of the customer that had ensured the survival of Markington's market-leading product. After the merger, rationalisation of the negative attitudes was repeatedly brought up against the truth as the customers expressed it through all levels of their contact with Markington. Sometimes, however, companies do things to 'keep the customers happy', hoping that the day will come when they stop doing them. Today's airline pilot is in the middle of just such a tussle.

Computers, or something like computers, have been part of the flying machine almost since Kitty Hawk. The first gyroscopes were introduced to help the efficiency of aircraft, and these soon developed into the early 'autopilots', enabling an aircraft to maintain course without the pilot's hands on the controls. The bomb aimers of the Second World War depended on these devices, and early rockets were managed by them, the primitive forerunners of today's computers in aircraft.

The first aircraft to use a computer to improve its performance and 'flyability' took off in 1958. The Apollo

Lunar Module of 1969 used an analog computer flight control system, widely referred to by now as about as intelligent as a modern washing machine, and all US space missions since have had computer flight control systems.

By the 1970s there were the first of many 'fly-by-wire' aircraft control systems appearing, removing the direct linkage from pilot to the aircraft. Today computers constantly adjust the flight controls to maintain the aircraft in flight and reply to the commands from the pilot. Some inherently unstable aircraft could never fly without their computers.

In the skies over the earth today aircraft are connected by radio and satellite link to a global information system that provides them with information on the weather, on other aircraft nearby and on their flight paths, and makes it possible for them to cross and re-cross the planet from airport apron to airport apron almost entirely automatically. Pilots seem all but redundant, and some airlines suggest that they are only there today to reassure the passengers. The pilots are less than grateful to be so regarded, and there have been walk-outs and strikes caused in no small part by the disagreement as to the long-term viability of these expensive employees.

But it is inevitable that at some time, somewhere in the world, an aircraft computer system, or an entire flight planning super-computer, will fail or – like HAL – go slightly insane. Then there will only be one person between the passengers and certain disaster. Indeed, if it were to happen in certain situations, such as the final approach to London Heathrow, over a city with more than seven million inhabitants, only the aircraft pilot might be able to prevent a horror that would glare from screens around the world in seconds, and in a moment of time destroy the airline and possibly many others.

Should that sequence of events ever occur, the pilot, who has now become widely seen as merely a hugely overpaid accessory doing less work most days than the cabin crew, is the most important person in the airline. The moment the computers fail, the amount their pilots earn per month, per year, per flight, will become totally unimportant. For at that time the only thing that will matter is that someone is immediately available with the knowledge that is needed. The same holds true of the heart surgeon and the firefighter and countless others in our society. When they are needed, the cost incurred to get them to that time and place, and to keep them there, is of no concern, for the alternative is disaster.

So it is with organisational change. When the challenge comes, it can lead to great disaster or great success, and that will depend on the knowledge available. The cost of that knowledge is not then for counting. Until the change begins, no one knows what knowledge will one day be needed. All that anyone can do is ensure that knowledge is constantly gathered, updated, recorded and retained.

Many organisations fail to do this. In the last decade of the twentieth century, many were lulled into a sense of false security by their technology. They learned to rely on their autopilots, and looked at the 'expensive' people they had. The response was to shed staff through a huge range of strategies – downsizing, restructuring, delayering and outsourcing. In place of the 'expensive', 'old' workforce, they employed fewer, cheaper staff who could run all the smoothly operating computer systems, doing only the tasks that were not automated. Respected and established industry names were abandoned for 'modern' ones, old relationships 'replaced', 'unproductive' activities closed down. After all, the autopilot was in control.

This destroys Recognition, one of the essentials of successful change. The new staff, employed as a cheaper resource, inevitably are less experienced in the business. For this reason they often fail to understand where the company is, even what it does, often with dramatic results. An example from the UK training sector illustrates this.

A new employee in a recently restructured training support organisation responded to a telephone call. The enquirer was seeking advice on the development of occupational standards for his industry. Previously, such a call would have been referred to an 'expensive' manager, but most of the expensive managers had been encouraged to take redundancy. Calls were now taken by 'customer service', and customer service staff were recruited from outside the industry. Not knowing sufficient about the totality of capability within the organisation, the employee responded with 'I don't think we could do that'. The caller went away. The caller had in fact been a representative of the UK's entire rail network, with a budget to match. The answer they had been given was factually and terribly wrong – the organisation had practically invented the type of occupational competence the caller was interested in. Amazingly, the skills were still available in the organisation. Finally – and tragically – not only had the new employee failed to recognise the importance of the enquiry, but failed also to take a note of the name or the number of the caller.

When enough of the organisation has been replaced or removed and it fails to recognise the truth, it is easy to construct false futures and to build a false Reality on the restrictions imposed by 'what we are doing now'. Eventually, a process of rationalisation may become so firmly embedded that the few experienced workers, the holders of the last vestiges of the heritage of corporate knowledge, are driven out, and with them the skills and experience that would have helped to create the necessary Reconciliation – or to put it another way, to get the organisation on track for the future.

8

Politics and truth

Making excuses: how is it excusable not to know what you don't know, but inexcusable to pretend that no one knows the things you don't want to know

Both Recognition of the truth of the present and Reality or the future can bring uncomfortable situations about. Too often they suggest a necessary Reconciliation that is too difficult, too costly, politically uncomfortable or such a dramatic change of direction that it is rejected. One such situation occurred a decade ago, but the situation is a common one. In it, the 'people in charge' felt forced to defend their failure to take the actions Recognition and Reality clearly demanded of them.

The politician on the TV screen was explaining it again, very firmly, very self-righteously. No, she wouldn't be resigning. No, she certainly had done nothing wrong. The interviewer completely missed the point, which, rationally, was that she hadn't done anything she should not have done. She had done everything she should have done. 'Surely', she was saying, 'you wouldn't have wanted me to do other than follow the appropriate procedures? That way lies anarchy. You cannot seriously be in favour of anarchy?' So, if the interviewer was not seriously proposing anarchy, no one could seriously have expected her to do differently. No blame could be attached to her. The interviewer obviously had to see that, 'No one knew it was going to happen.'

This was the usual and wonderful political argument. If no one knew it was going to happen, no one could do anything about it before it happened. So when it did happen, no one could be blamed. This argument was also, despite its frequent use by politicians, an absolute untruth.

The small island under discussion, a former colonial possession, had been almost wiped out by an enormous volcanic explosion in which hundreds, possibly a thousand, of its people had been killed or made homeless. A huge international aid effort was immediately mounted, and as always happens, problems arose. Supplies were delayed, transport was in the wrong place, politics intervened. The world's TV arrived there ahead of the aid, and the horror filled the TV screens of billions of viewers who reacted with anger. The typical view was expressed loudly along the lines of: 'It's five days, and we still haven't got the aid in. People are dying because our governments are so slow. We are the rich world, and we can't get to the poor world when they most need us. Why weren't we ready? Where is the guilty politician?'

The guilty politician is perhaps the one who is now saying on TV, 'no one knew it was going to happen'. But of course they did. The kingfisher had indeed flown by. Their scientists had warned for years that the volcano would one day blow. There had been rumblings in 1897, 1933 and 1966. Geology showed that there had been eruptions in prehistoric times, and certain of the lava flows on the surface of the island were apparently quite young, or 'young' in geological terms anyway. The islanders had strong traditions which included allusions to the volcano blowing. The seismologists listening around the world had heard the warning noises for years. People knew it would happen.

But the people who knew, the scientists, were powerless to prevent the tragedy, and the people who they were able to tell were the wrong people to take the steps for the inevitable aftermath. When they heard of the Reality, the politicians decided that as the scientists disagreed about exactly what to expect and couldn't supply their data in the nice, clear and definite terms that the politicians required (in part as a buffer against responding to common sense, a technique common to all governments), the information could be ignored. It was not of immediate, popular use to the elected politicians to know that the eruption was very definitely going to happen within the next half century, or maybe the next 200 years. There are no votes to be had in expensive precautions taken too soon. And so, when it came, the politicians could claim they couldn't have been expected to know it would happen, 'to know' meaning 'not for certain, not then, not like that'.

The terrorist outrage, the epidemic, the collapse of a major corporation, the flood, the earthquake – someone somewhere always 'knows' they are going to happen. They may not be precise in the details or their knowledge may be disbelieved or others may not accept what is known. Sometimes ignoring such knowledge is a grand self-deception and those with responsibility take a chance on the knowledge not becoming important when they have the command. It is almost a defining characteristic of politicians that they can refuse to recognise the truth, to pour scorn on the Reality, in order to avoid at all costs the discomfort of Reconciliation. An incredulous world yet again watches their every interview, each enforced public performance, their patent self-deception, when the results of their refusal lead inevitably, eventually, to a failure of leadership.

9

Expensive ignorance

'I want to teach the world to spring!'
How there is no such thing as useless
information, only information whose use
has yet to be established

In 2003 Dasani purified water, a product with an almost infinite profit margin, lost Coca-Cola an estimated £40 million, and the company's reputation was severely damaged by the fiasco.

Dasani is America's second largest brand of 'bottled water'. The term 'bottled water' is critical to the disaster in England. In America, leading brands of bottled water are purified water from the public water supply with extra 'flavouring' minerals added.

In Europe, the market is quite different. At the top end are the hugely respected natural mineral waters such as Perrier, Harrogate Spa and San Pellegrino. There is also a whole strata of lesser waters, known as spring waters, which include most supermarket own brands. There is almost no market in Britain or Europe for what, by European definition, Dasani was: 'table water'.

But there was something else that Coca-Cola did not know which almost anyone in Britain could have told them.

Their UK factory was in Sidcup, London, and they took water from the local water supply, treating it and bottling it. Less than ten miles away is Peckham.

Peckham is legendary in Britain as the fictional home of one Del Boy Trotter and his family of barely legal traders and small-time entrepreneurs. Also legendary in Britain is an episode of the TV programme Del starred in, in which he set up a production line to sell 'Peckham Spring' water – in fact, bottled tap water. With, as they say in the reviews, hilarious consequences.

So when the people of Britain learned of the new Coca-Cola product, the immediate response was derision, followed rapidly by disbelief that Coca-Cola could even consider trying to sell 'Sidcup Spring' water. Dasani was doomed from the start. When later the company discovered that it couldn't be sold in Europe as 'pure' (it had additives) and then accidentally ran foul of the regulations on bromate levels, it was indefinitely withdrawn.

Coca-Cola, it seemed, knew well enough what they wanted to achieve: they wanted to be one of the top selling bottled waters in Britain and Europe. They had made their investment plans on the basis of where they wanted Dasani to be in the bottled water market. They knew exactly how to produce bottled water from the public water supply. They knew how to distribute it. They knew how to market an international brand. So why did they fail?

Because they didn't know enough about where they were starting. They didn't know about the British and their uneasy relationship with bottled waters. They didn't seem know about the strong European tradition of famous mineral and spring waters. They critically didn't know about Del Boy Trotter. If they had, they would have realised that they were attempting to produce a product in a location that would immediately attract public derision.

It is possible that if the Coca-Cola board had spent 40 minutes watching an old British TV comedy programme they could have saved £40 million. It is inevitable that had they listened to the workers building the new plant, or to the locals in the pubs, they would have encountered the information they needed to establish Recognition. But it wasn't the sort of information they wanted to obtain, and it certainly wasn't the way they wanted to obtain it.

Secundi and the Dasani story

In this case an initial failure of Recognition created cumulative damage. The Coca-Cola company is huge, long-established, rich and multinational. In establishing the Secundi coefficient for the Dasani disaster, it is necessary to explore the relationships between the functions of the top line of the coefficient calculation.

The company undoubtedly knew how to market a branded product. They knew how to finance and open a bottling plant. They knew how to advertise, distribute, promote and extend a product. They should have had a Recognition score of 10. But it wasn't like that.

Because they didn't know the killer facts – or if they did know them they rationalised them away, perhaps the most serious aspect of a lack of Recognition. So the importance in the situation of the facts they didn't know had far more weight than the facts they did know. They didn't apparently even address the issues of the legality of their intended label, claiming to be 'pure'. They didn't do the market research on British waters, to discover that no one, not one supermarket, not one importer, had ever sold 'table water' in the market. And not to understand the story of 'Peckham Spring', not to factor it in, was so serious that a score of 3 is generous for Recognition.

With a score of 3 for Recognition, although the company knew all the technicalities, the Reality was that they should not be trying to launch this product from this base. It was pointless to try. That they went ahead meant they had little grasp of Reality. Surely on their visits to Britain they had become aware of what the British tabloid press was capable, yet they imagined the great weight of 'Coke' would always carry the day. Again, the nature of the missing understanding outweighs everything they sought to achieve. A Reality score of 3 again is generous.

There was therefore little point in planning a route, but they did so. They based their Reconciliation on false premises and relied entirely on their industrial and market muscle. But as it was the wrong product, in the wrong market with the wrong characteristics, all the technical competence was useful, but not relevant to the main problem they were going to face. A Reconciliation score of 2.

Top line: Recognition 3 + Reality 3 + Reconciliation 2 = 8

The Secundi coefficient was therefore 8 divided by 30, a value of 0.26. Failure was almost inevitable.

10

Radical change

*'Tell it to the birdies' – how radical change
is any change we cannot respond to
incrementally, and the near death of some
cash register makers*

Many companies have failed because they have not understood the Reality of radical change. The world in which all possible threats were easily seen and minor changes to a company's products or services would serve to maintain a market position is virtually gone. There are still a few organisations that think they can continue indefinitely to survive through incremental change, but they are both few and foolish. They are like a flock of birds.

It had settled in the northeast corner of the field, a huge grey stain on the summer green of the freshly mowed grass. The clouds scuttling high above explained its presence, for birds seek shelter on the ground and inland as storms threaten. The flock was maybe a couple of thousand strong and quite a rare sight in that part of the world.

Perhaps because of the time of day, or the look of the weather, few people saw the flock. One man walking across the diagonal pathway, perhaps on his way home from town for he carried a bag from a well-known store, noticed the flock. Noticing it, he slowed, then halted. He was perhaps puzzled, or maybe he was a bird-watcher, or simply curious by nature, for he diverted from the footpath and walked slowly across the field towards the flock, as if trying to gain a better view or to identify the birds.

As he walked towards it the flock at first seemed unmoved. He approached the back of the flock hesitantly. Then, as he was maybe fifty feet from the flock a strange thing happened. As if on a signal, the entire rear section of the flock rose in the air. The man halted, watching the several hundred birds wheeling into the sky. The rest of the flock remained stationary on the ground, but now the back rows of birds were further from the man. Then, again as one, the birds in the air ceased their wheeling, and settled down to land again. They landed on the opposite side of the flock from the man, forming a new front section.

The birds having settled, the man moved forwards once more. Again, as he was maybe fifty feet from the rearmost birds, they lifted into the air, wheeled noisily overhead, and in a minute settled once more as the new front lines of the flock. The man seemed fascinated by the curious phenomenon, and continued to walk towards the flock. Again and again the rearmost and the foremost sections of the flock shuffled, the flock remaining to all appearances the same. Except that as it rearranged itself, it slowly crept across the field. It seemed unperturbed.

In the far corner of the field a second walker had appeared. On a lead next to him, a dog. A large, long-legged dog with a russet coat, straining on the leash. The owner pulled it towards him, bent briefly over its neck and straightened up. As the owner reached his upright stance, the dog was already far gone, loping towards the flock, not barking, simply moving faster and faster, heading not for the rear, but for the very centre. Just as it was about to reach it, the entire flock, as one, rose into the air and scattered, squealing. Some turned towards the town, some for the trees around the fields, some upwind, some downwind. It did not form a mass in the sky and it did not settle again.

The first man, who had been slowly rearranging the flock by his measured approaches, stood and scanned the sky, then searched the field's extremes. He found no sign of the flock. He turned back towards the path, shopping swinging by his side, and briskly hurried along to catch up his lost minutes. The dog catapulted on long legs back to its owner, who now had a ball in his hand, ready to throw. The field itself, its surface barely rippled by the unsettlingly urgent breeze, seemed to have been left unchanged. The flock, although calmly resettling itself after each small perceived threat, had failed to survive the one sudden, major change in its world and ceased to exist.

Which is pretty much the story of the mechanical cash register. Even today, the cash drawer with its dividers to hold different types of notes and coins has been a common feature of small shops all around the world. It probably first appeared in the eighteenth century, but as business volume grew due to the Industrial Revolution and increasing urbanisation, shopkeepers became more and more aware of its limitations. In addition to the temptation the cash drawer held for shop assistants there was a growing need for quick and accurate summaries of daily transactions. Because there was no way to easily audit transactions, dishonest cashiers frequently supplemented their wages by removing cash. This was said to be the reason for so many prices being set a cent or penny below the next main value, such as $9.99, to make 'fiddling' show up at the end of the day; clearly their bosses didn't expect their staff to be such mental arithmeticians as to be able to both fiddle the tills and ensure an end-of-day matching balance in the cash drawer!

The cash register was invented in 1879 by James Ritty, a saloonkeeper in Dayton, Ohio. Saloons, with their combination of noise, alcohol and cash passing across the counter, were notoriously difficult places for owners to control the cash flow. Ritty's machine was a mechanical counter with all the essentials that survive in cash registers until this day. It had different keys for different values, a bell to ring up sales (so that supervisors would know the cash drawer was open) and a mechanism for showing all the key presses during a day. This was the machine that was to launch NCR, originally the National Cash Register company, in 1884. Strangely, the huge success of NCR was to lead ultimately to the end of the product it was built on, for in 1906 NCR began to market the machines to Japan, setting up a Japanese division in 1920.

Soon the cash register was capable of providing an audit trail of daily transactions, a customer count, detailed amounts rung up and cumulative totals. It became possible to identify individual product sales, which enabled special promotions, individual incentive schemes for shopworkers and the first collection of quantitative market data. This was achieved with pure mechanics, relying on gears and levers, and with new features (variable sales tax calculators, currency changes) being added as they were required. The cash register remained pretty much as it was originally invented and was manufactured in much the same way for over a century.

As a result the big makers became lazy, with responses to market needs being produced as they always had been, incrementally. When the United Kingdom changed over to a decimal-based currency, they at first simply provided labels to cover up the old currency values and then, using the old mechanical techniques, produced properly decimal machines. After all, they had captive customers and the only real issue was market share.

As well as being the year that the United Kingdom converted to decimal currency, 1971 was the year that NCR Japan produced the world's first electronic cash register, the NCR 230. Based not on mechanics but on the new technology of computing logic, this machine was in time to wipe out all but a few of the companies making traditional cash registers. And as the world moved into a phase of dearer labour, the new technology cash registers had a characteristic that was to ultimately make them the survivors – they could be manufactured entirely by machine.

The mechanical cash register makers soldiered on for a decade. They responded in their conventional ways. The workforces were reduced to cut costs. The designs were simplified. New materials were introduced. Components were redesigned, outsourced, then eliminated. Prices were cut, marginally, when necessary. Special offers were used to retain market share. In short, they responded to the threat of major change with an inadequate incremental response.

It is safe to bet that during this period, some of the accountants and engineers in these companies stopped using their slide rules to do calculations. Instead, they would have started using the new Casio FX-1 or the HP 35, the world's first 'affordable' pocket calculators. If they had spent a moment browsing in their local office stationery shop, they might have noticed that slide rules, a near essential tool for calculations since their invention in 1622, had vanished like a flock of birds chased away by a dog.

11

Knowledge

*The need-to-know principle and how
we survive it, and 'one more time: how
do we wreck good ideas?'*

The need-to-know principle is a wonderful thing. People should only know what they need to, all else is superfluous, and maybe dangerous. Sometimes people don't really want to know some things, and anyway, sometimes the information is of little use or value for most of the time.

Knowledge is a strange commodity. There are some things that we know that we know, although we often forget. That isn't the same as not knowing it. This can be called the 'quiz reaction'. The quiz reaction is what happens when the person on the TV quiz doesn't know the answer but we do! Before the question was asked, we never would have remembered we knew it, but we did. The person on the quiz show doesn't know it, but they know that someone else knows it.

This matters in the world we inhabit as individuals, because we rely on this odd feature of knowledge. We go to the doctor, the lawyer, the tax adviser because we know both that we don't have certain knowledge, but that we know that they have it. At the desk or the consulting table, they also know that we don't know 'the knowledge', which is what they are selling us, in the most useful and profitable package.

Inevitably, if we don't know something, we come to the question of the truth of what we are told. If I know that I don't know something, how do I know that what I am told is the truth? If I knew that, I wouldn't have needed to ask. As individuals we have three answers to this problem. The first is to accept without question, based on trust. This works fine when the question is, 'does this road take me out of town?', and the person we ask seems confident of the reply they give, and we usually feel safe accepting it.

Our second technique is to double check. When a valuer tells us that our house is worth a lot less than we thought, or the house we want to buy is worth a lot more than we want to pay, our response is often to ask for a second opinion from a different expert. Sometimes we ask for a third opinion.

Our third response is to check what the answer might be before we ask the question. This is the 'used car strategy' – before we go to trade in our motor we check in the small ads about what level of price to expect. We find comparable models in similar condition, and check their prices, calculating the buying-in price from that. We may even go to a couple of used car dealers we don't intend to give the business to, just so that when we get the offer from our choice of dealer, we can then decide if it's likely to be about right.

Some organisations seem to work differently. For a start they often don't worry about what they don't know, because they think the only thing that matters is what they do know.

If they know how to make the product, how to sell the product, how to service the product, that is all they need to know. They can, after all, always find out how their competitors do pretty much the same things, although even from this they don't expect to find out much they don't already know. For this reason they almost never have a department, a person, whose responsibility it is to find out what is going on in the wider world, to ask the questions that seem unnecessary, and to find out the things that the organisation doesn't know it doesn't know, and doesn't realise yet that it needs to know.

The marketing people can find out about marketing the products better, the research department can research how to make better products, the manufacturing team can find better ways to make the better products, but who is there to say, with the authority of knowledge, 'we need to start making an entirely different product'?

Removing this organisational blindfold is a challenge that often is resisted. The board may decide that they want to be more efficient, leaner, smarter, cheaper, bigger or faster, and hire a consultant. The consultant arrives and does what consultants do – asks questions, applies comparators, reaches conclusions and in due course presents a report to the board. The board listens politely and achieves a degree of Recognition.

Then they look at the implications, the Reality, of the report. They begin to work out the Reconciliation, and seeing the truth, begin to rationalise the position. They apply the standard tools: the wrecking ball for new ideas, the list of ways to stop new ideas in their tracks. Together they decide that they didn't want to know the things they didn't know. The matter is resolved. The consultant is paid. The report is filed. The board goes home.

Ways to block a good idea and prevent change

- We tried that once and it didn't work.
- Our people won't like it.
- It costs too much.
- It's too expensive.
- It's too difficult.
- It's not the way we do things here.
- If it isn't broken don't fix it.
- If it's such a good idea someone else would have done it already.
- People aren't ready for it.
- Let's think about it for a while longer.
- We've never done it before.
- Show us someone who's done it already.

12

Taking stock of life

How life refuses to recognise the
compartments we try to impose on it
– life just gets on with being life

All life is change. All around us are our life's projects and processes, and all are at some specific stage of transition. The potted plants outside the window remain stubbornly below their compost, corms only slowly awakening. We know that as the days tick on, they will change into greenery and flowering plants before dying back as autumn arrives, and with that we shall have achieved our 'pretty patio' project for this year.

While that process continues we will perhaps move through a period when we work with the patio doors open, and the days will get brighter and warmer, and then cooler and darker. And all of this will go on whether we are at home or at work while it happens, or whether home is where we work, or whether we sometimes seem to be living at our workplace.

All these processes will constantly interact, and we do not know what the effect will be on any of them of the success of the others. Will the open patio door being open have an impact on the work or the way we work? Will the plants blossoming affect our thinking? Or the thinking of others, who in turn will have an impact on us? And what other projects will start, develop and end in the same period?

It is all a jumble to us. We do not know how many of our life projects are running, because mostly we can keep only half a dozen in mind at a time. Each of those is at a point that we can describe. Or at least we think we can describe the point we are at. Which is remarkably similar to what our work looks like, with its tussle of constantly evolving and changing major and minor projects.

Actually we can only describe where we think we are, in life as in work. We know that the project labelled 'empty the garage' is about half way to success, but really we don't know if it will be completed. We are perhaps quite determined, but another life project, such as 'family', 'marriage' or 'money' may interfere.

So to the projects at work, we have no idea of the Reality. We only know where we think we might be in these projects. For them to succeed, for us to emerge from the projects of our lives safely and happily, it would be useful to know what at least one other person thinks that they know. But we don't really want to ask. So we can't truly know where we stand.

It seems the chances of our life projects succeeding are mixed. It would perhaps help if we knew properly what all our projects are, and whereabouts we are in each. For sure, in some of them it would be better if we weren't starting from where we are. But given that we are starting from where we are, we need at least to know where 'here' is. What we need is a process that helps us to understand the cumulative interaction and impact of all these projects. We need to carry out a Recognition, Reality, Reconciliation process on ourselves.

13

The dangers of dogmas

*To change is easy. To change for the better –
that is the challenge. A story of a change
process with too much Resolution and too little
Reality – the UK's personal pensions strategy*

Sometimes governments create a terrible conflict between the results of their Recognition (situation analysis), the Reality (prognosis) and their chosen Reconciliation (solution). As we have seen, when these are together underpinned by the huge degree of Resolution of a sitting government with a powerful regulatory capability, chaos can result. Such is the potential outcome of the British government's attempts to address what it perceived to be a pensions 'time bomb' (a term much favoured by pressure groups inside and outside government) in the 1980s.

Since the UK Liberal government of 1906–14 introduced state pensions, there had developed three financial strands to retirement income for UK citizens. These were public funds, employer pensions and personal savings. Since 1945 the UK has provided a 'basic' state pension funded by employer and employee payroll deductions, the value of which is a factor of the number of years in which a worker has contributed, regardless of earnings. It alone does not provide sufficient retirement income and the employer-provided pension, based on contributions by both employers and their employees, became an important supplement when the government instituted the State Earnings Related Pension Scheme (SERPS). This was funded by additional contributions, and promised retirees an extra 25 per cent of their average annual wages for their most highly paid twenty years of employment. SERPS was compulsory unless the employer provided a pension plan whose benefits equalled or exceeded those of SERPS. This combination of promise and compulsion was to sow the seeds of chaos.

As in many other areas, the Second World War had seriously interfered with the capability of the state to service its commitments by creating a baby boom in the immediate postwar years. The extravagant thanks and promises made to returning servicemen began to come home to roost, and the state contribution to all activities, from education to health, social security, public services and retirement income, came under enormous pressure. In 1986 the UK government under Margaret Thatcher was a Conservative one, with a range of often aggressive 'modernising' policies. One key policy was reducing government spending through privatisation, a move intended to reduce the taxation burden and thus help to create a new generation of Conservative voters. In accordance with this belief, they began a process intended to curtail the government share of total pension funding in future years. As the Conservative Party was also funded substantially by employers, the strategy was designed also to reduce employer contributions to pension funds.

To create an apparently virtuous social and political justification for this move, the policy was sold as both 'shrinking the role of government' and 'increasing individual choice' over savings and investments. The policy vehicle was 'Personal Pensions', and to launch and maintain it some forceful measures were introduced. One was the reduction of the value of SERPS to make personal pensions seem more attractive. This meant that employees who had paid into SERPS under compulsion for more than a decade saw the government promises broken and a worrying gap in their retirement income appearing unless they took up the personal pension offerings.

Another lever was a tax incentive to purchase these less attractive, riskier personal pensions, many of which had fees consuming up to 20 per cent of a worker's contributions, without any balancing contribution from their employer. But probably most seriously, the firms permitted to offer personal pension plans were allowed for several years to continue making extravagant – and in hindsight potentially untruthful – claims about their pension products. Together these measures and this strategy created a situation which encouraged many of the holders of secure existing employer pensions to abandon these in favour of riskier, personal pensions of lesser value. By 1993 5.7 million employees had opted for personal pensions, at huge profit to the companies selling the schemes. By 1997 there were some 10 million personal pension plans sold.

In 1997 the problems had already begun to emerge. A report by the United Kingdom's Office of Fair Trading noted that already, over half a million personal pension plans had been investigated for having been misrepresented to their buyers. Fifty thousand of these cases had been reviewed, and

12,000 claims for compensation had been payed. Estimates for the total cost of review and compensation grew, and it was obvious that these could in time easily exceed £20 billion. The government had in fact 'saved' £7 billion in reduced SERPS liabilities by spending over £20 billion on rebates and incentives. The situation that emerged was that the costs now far exceeded the financial 'risk' that had caused the Conservative government to adopt and drive through the strategy so forcefully.

While the government saw its liabilities actually rising, with a consequent need to introduce many new measures to support pensioners, personal pensions made fortunes for the companies on whom the government had sought to offload its traditional responsibilities. A report for the World Bank estimated that the raft of fees and costs could take an average of 43 per cent of the value of an individual's personal pension account over the course of a typical, 40-year working career. Yet since 1995, profit margins in the top sellers of personal pensions were said to exceed 22 per cent.

It is difficult to forecast what kind of retirement UK pensioners can now expect. There is clear doubt that existing personal pensions are sufficient to assure a comfortable retirement, especially for lower-paid workers. The incoming Labour government in the late 1990s, with a huge degree of Resolution, set up a 'stakeholder pension' intended mainly for lower-paid employees which failed to make a substantial impact, as these workers in particular are often unable to make additional contributions. A range of benefits for pensioners (visibly getting worse and worse off) had to be introduced, with the 'minimum income guarantee' (difficult to obtain and means tested) making saving into pension plans even less attractive to those who could estimate their retirement income, as they saw that such savings were increasingly counterproductive because they added little to income but removed future entitlement to state benefits and rebates.

One further consequence became apparent in 2004, when the UK's Alliance & Leicester bank, together with the think-tank 'The Centre for Future Studies', reported that as many as six million British people had already made tentative plans to move abroad by 2020. Four million of those moving were expected to be of retirement age. The three reasons given to the researchers were dwindling pensions, workplace stress and the poor quality of daily life in the UK. An estimated one million Britons had already retired abroad. If indeed six million Britons feel forced to move abroad, the economy as a whole would feel the shocks.

Perhaps the Thatcher government was correct in their Recognition of the problem they had. They may have interpreted the Reality, based on the best prognoses, as well as they could. But the Resolution they chose was informed by a number of overriding political positions, and as a result was not the ideal, or even the best available. Like the early navigators facing strange new oceans, the errors compounded and took them further and further off course. But with iron determination, the government was able to drive through their changes against all opposition. The force they used through taxation and incentives, and by enabling the market to engage in the business of government and then staying aloof as the early problems emerged, has led to a potential pensions situation which could haunt their successors. As the increasingly vocal, politically active, baby boomers approach their own retirement, visible 'pensioner poverty' in one of the world's richest countries will surely force a sudden, very radical change on whatever government is in power.

14

Change masters

*How 'change masters' make perfect
cakes, and why we don't*

The world was probably introduced to the term 'change
master' in 1983 when Rosabeth Moss Kanter published her
book, *The Change Masters: Innovation and Entrepreneurship in the American Corporation.*[1] In it she introduces us to
her views of the reasons why people resist change. She looks
at the fear of change, of loss of control, of uncertainty about
the future and of the consequences of change on the
individuals involved.

Scan the advertisements in any major recruitment section
of a newspaper or sector magazine and it is a fair chance
you will find them replete with references to 'managing
change'. It is as if the much sought-after managers of change
hold some special toolkit of skills, have a particular set of
abilities and attitudes that enable them to transform any
organisation they work for. But change isn't really like that.
Maybe it does help to be familiar with forcefield analysis.
Perhaps a nodding acquaintance with the Gantt chart is
useful. It may be that change in some organisations can
naturally be described by using the Ishikawa diagram. But
there is no one, right way to manage change. And certainly
no recipe for leadership though times of change.

Delia Smith is an internationally renowned cookery author and presenter of TV cookery programmes. Around the world there are thousands of lunch and dinner parties daily which are partly or wholly based on recipes from the 10 million Delia Smith cookery books already sold. With Delia at your elbow, you can do no wrong in the kitchen. Or so it would seem.

For Delia knows exactly what she has to her hand. She can list the ingredients, their quality, reliability and weights or volumes. Her oven is at the right temperature. Her pans are the right size. There is no error possible. Before she shoots a TV show, a team of assistants have made sure that everything is as it should be. When Delia looks around her TV kitchen, she sees the Reality. Exactly as she expects to see it.

When we cook ourselves, it isn't like that. We think we have what we need but may have to make some substitutions. The oven is probably about the right temperature, give or take a bit. We don't have the size of pan that Delia uses but one that will probably do. We would like the 'assistants' to get out of the way. When we look around, we see a different Reality. But it is our Reality.

Delia knows what she wants to achieve. She has it written down. She knows what it will look like, exactly, because she has seen it before. She knows what it will taste like, exactly, because she has tasted it before. And she knows how long it will take, exactly, because she has made it before.

When we start to cook, we have only an idea of what it will look like, because we have never made it before. We hope it will taste good, but we haven't tried it before so it's a bit of a chance. We hope the book we are relying on is right, because we have a limited amount of time and we've not cooked it before.

Delia whisks swiftly and surely through the process. She knows how to beat that, how to blend this, how to slice those, how to skin these. She moves assuredly, all the while telling us what she is doing. Not what she is trying to do, but what she is doing. She does it right, every time, because she knows exactly how to.

When we cook we move unsurely, not knowing quite how to achieve the result. We have to learn to beat that, how to blend this, how to slice those and how to skin these. We haven't done it before, and we rely on the book at our elbow to guide us. Some of it we clearly get wrong, but we haven't done it before

Delia has done it all easily, smoothly, assuredly. She has managed her change confidently, supremely, exactly. We have had to work much harder, but we get there, or somewhere close to there, in the end. We have learned from Delia, but our worlds will always be different, and only we know just how different.

Note

1. Rosabeth Moss Kanter (1983/1985) *The Change Masters: Innovation and Entrepreneurship in the American Corporation*. New York: Free Press.

15

The continuity of change

How we never reach the end of change, and how Nokia made mobile phones a fashion item

There was a feeling of headiness, a slight dizziness, a hint of unreality, as the climber looked skywards to the summit ahead. It was quite distinct, and not a trace of mist in the sky.

He then turned and looked down, behind him. Like a toy in the cupped hands of the earth was the glimmer of the lake from whose shore he had started. There, beside the long, low stone building was the car park for the visitor centre, and just out of sight behind a rock outcrop on the side of the hill was the outside cafeteria he had sat in to make last minute preparations for this climb.

Not that it was a serious climb in the sense that a true climber would use the word. It was not Andean or Himalayan in its demands, either physical or mental. Still, he thought, the peaks were no molehills either, no pushover, no easy ride. This was no gentle stroll. He hefted the daypack more securely to his shoulders and turned again to the path upwards. He was more than a bit out of breath, and well aware that his legs were tired, which he had expected. But he had somewhere he needed to go, and so they were required to keep going.

The challenge wasn't conventional. There was no bet, no obligation, except to himself. He had been through a rough patch, life had been tougher than was pleasant, he had faced problems and, with the help of friends and support, come through. But he felt at risk. He'd shed old habits, he'd re-educated his metabolism, reworked his surroundings, refound his way in life and at work. But it wasn't quite enough. He needed a life marker. In short, having recognised his position, deduced the Reality, he had worked out the Reconciliation that was needed. This walk was his test of Resolution, except that unlike a test, failure was not an option.

He had come to the challenge by chance. As he had motored through the pass earlier that year, making a leisurely trip to a conference, he had stopped at the roadside and left the driving seat in response to a glimpse of a large raptor soaring high on the current of air above his car. As he tracked the hawk with his binoculars, his glasses had been drawn repeatedly to the ridge opposite, and unexpectedly he had said to himself, 'There it is'.

So the summit had become the objective, and the next few months had been spent preparing and taking stock. To get him from the driving seat of the saloon, shirted and suited, slightly portly, not very fit, to a medium-height summit was a challenge. But it had to be met. There was no doubt it had to be done. There wasn't a substitute, no plan B. There was no mortgaged deal to buy it out. It was there, starkly stony. Inevitable.

Now at last, the final few hundred feet lay ahead. Strangely, the path was not steeper, the challenge not greater. Indeed, the challenge at the base had been greater. It was the commencement of the journey that was the hard bit, for he had realised that he could not, once the path was taken, turn back. It was to be. It was to spell the end of that phase of his life.

Five steps to the summit, and he stood easily on it, panting a bit, aching, but not surprised. He had first seen the peak, determined that he needed to reach it, prepared himself for the journey, set his course and now had achieved it. He felt proud, satisfied, maybe slightly smug to be standing there as the gentle wind tugged at his clothing.

Strangely, however, it now didn't feel like he'd reached the end.

Successful companies never reach the end. As they reach each new 'summit' they see the next. In 1865 the world was quite busy with the usual order of things. Enough was going on for most people. Slavery was abolished in the United States, Abraham Lincoln was assassinated and Joseph Lister had the first inkling that surgery could be a lot safer if it was carried out under antiseptic conditions. The first books of Leo Tolstoy's *War and Peace* series appeared, and in a small Finnish town a paper mill opened. It had seen a market and, given the main natural resources of Finland, set out to capitalise on Europe's growing need for the basic tools of communication and export their products to Russia, Britain and France.

As the factory grew, it found it had surplus electricity from the hydroelectric scheme that powered the pulp plant. Soon it had a neighbouring rubber factory with an appetite for this surplus power. Through the 1920s, while Al Capone ran his mob in Chicago and the 'Roaring Twenties' in the USA whirled by in a frenzy of home-made whisky, speakeasies, flappers, gangsters and crime, the small town of Nokia first saw its name appear as a brand on goods from rubber bands to tyres. Nokia was still producing the tools the world needed for commerce.

By the end of the Second World War the Finnish Cable Works, providing essential equipment for telegraphy, was added to the Nokia stable, staking a firm claim in transmission, telegraph and telephone networks as commerce developed around the world. The transistor had been invented in 1947, but as yet it had no wide consumer applications. In 1967, a century after that first factory, the three companies were merged to form the Nokia Group, still with a mission to supply the essential tools of commerce. Now the tools were different, and by the end of the century they would be almost unrecognisable. But Nokia's leaders still planned to make its money by supplying them.

So it was that while the world was repairing its electro-mechanical analogue switches in the fast-expanding telecommunications sector, Nokia, with an eye to the very first mobile networks, began developing digital switches for the next generation of transmission systems. The first was launched in 1981, while the world was watching the inaugural flight of the space shuttle or playing Pacman.

Nokia largely let its competitors fight it out for the first generation of clumsy, heavy and unreliable analogue handsets. While the early contenders fought it out in the new telephony market, Nokia was quietly working towards the inevitable arrival of the second generation of digital handsets, and the arrival of a Global System for Mobile

Communications (GSM). In 1992, the year that George H. Bush had an unfortunate dinner accident in Japan and Europe signed up to the Maastricht Treaty, Nokia decided to divest itself of all its non-core activities and concentrate on mobile telephony. It had already seen that the new generation phones would attract new users who would have a different relationship with their handsets but would still need to communicate.

It was not mistaken. The Nokia 2100 phone, expected to sell 500,000 units, sold 20 million, and a generation was hooked, turning the handset from a business tool to a fashion item and creating the handset replacement market. Later, Nokia were to cunningly turn a manufacturing necessity into a market opportunity – simplifying the construction of the handset meant that it was possible to remove the plastic fascia. Soon, Nokia customers would be offered a range of alternative fascias that they could purchase – the fashion handset had arrived.

A company that started serving the communication needs of a world of 1.3 billion people now serves the communication needs of over 1.3 billion mobile phone users. Through each year since its foundation the company's leaders had watched and recognised the world in which they operated, worked out what that would mean, and plotted their route to Reconciliation. As they reached each fresh summit, like all the world's best companies they looked around, understood the Reality of their position, plotted a new a course that would take them to the next achievement and carried out their plans with Resolution.

16

Why imposed Reality fails

How it's better to listen properly before you decide what to do

The truth of Reality is that it comes out of full Recognition. It is the inevitable consequence, not a position imposed for other purposes. It is no use claiming that your organisation's Reality is inevitable if it is the result of opinions imposed through dogma or convenience. The result of imposing rather than identifying a Reality is that although it does not make failure inevitable, it will mean a struggle, and no matter how resolved the organisation's leaders may be, the struggle will show in stark light that the Reality was false and harden opposition to all the changes, no matter how virtuous some of the objectives may have seemed.

The guest on the radio consumer show was being very determined. He was explaining to an apparently baffled host why the world had no choice but to embrace the technology of the new 'Chip and PIN' cards. These were the new plastic credit and debit cards carrying a tiny electronic circuit, or chip, which held information to validate the identity of the user. The PIN (Personal Identification Number) entered at the transaction point by the customer had to be the same as the one embedded on the chip. In Reality, it was old technology.

PINs had been invented in the 1960s, and in Britain first used for cashpoint machines by Barclay's Bank. Chips had been around for over a decade, an entire era in technology.

'Make no mistake,' the guest was making pounding, table-thumping noises audible to listeners across the land, 'this is what you will have to do if you want to shop next year; there is no choice.' The host made amazed noises. The new technology wasn't, she said, going exactly smoothly, was it? 'Mere teething troubles,' blustered her guest.

Then the calls began to flood in from the 13 million listeners to the station. First on air was a disabled woman, with a disabled husband, who pointed out that she couldn't use the keypads herself, and recently had to stop getting money from ATM machines after repeatedly having her card swallowed. Her husband had an illness that meant he couldn't remember numbers. She would need to continue using the old signature system. On the day of the broadcast, one in five people in the United Kingdom had a registered long-term disability, and the specialist charities said that many were expected to be unable to use the PIN machines and their little keypads.

Another caller came on air telling of standing in a queue while the person at the till entered his new PIN number slowly, copying from a slip of paper, and audibly saying each number as he found it on the keypad. Wasn't this, the caller asked, just a mugger's charter? After all, at least it took some degree of skill and practice to forge a signature from a stolen card, but none at all to enter the stolen PIN, either seen, heard or simply beaten out of the card's rightful owner. The guest said there were obviously some people who would find it hard to get used to, but everybody would have to learn their new PIN and keep them secret. On the day of the broadcast, according to the bank and card issuers' own websites, the single most common problem people had with cards was having too many PINs, so that they had to write them down to be able to use their cards.

A third caller told of the insecurity and inconvenience of the new PIN pads. He was the owner of a small, typical corner store, there was nowhere in his shop where a keypad could be installed so that other customers couldn't see a shopper entering their PIN number. What was he expected to do, he asked, paint a line on the floor, or make his customers wait by the freezer until he let them up to the counter one at a time? The banks' apologist ridiculed the idea that PIN pads were insecure, and was sure that even small shops would find the change easy to implement. Anyway, he said, they would have to install the PIN pads, because that was the way it was going to be, the banks had spoken. The host selected the next caller.

He was a British consultant calling in from Spain after listening to the programme over the Internet. He told how Spain had the new PIN keypads, but he was never allowed to use his without also showing his passport. The supermarkets apparently had found that stolen cards often came with stolen PINs. The host thanked him, and quickly selected the last caller without passing to the guest for comment; it seemed superfluous to make that point again.

The last caller asked why the country was being put to all this trouble for a second-rate scheme, when in a very few years proper biometric cards would be widely available?

After all, successful trials had been held in Japan the year before, and even the UK government had decided to go directly to biometric for ID cards. He himself had bought a fingerprint recognition system for his computer for $35.00 a week or two before. Rather than a short-term experiment with Chip and PIN cards, shouldn't the banks wait for some properly secure technology? Wouldn't customers just be saddled with this second-rate, less secure system for years while the banks recouped the costs of the scheme?

The banks' champion was incandescent, scathing. Why were all these callers protesting? What bit of the solution didn't they understand? Didn't they realise they were part of the problem? The solution was as he stated it, and Chip and PIN was here now, and they would just have to do what they were told and stop whining. They had to learn their PINs, not write them down, and the system was foolproof, utterly secure. They just had to stop struggling and let the banks have their way.

Within two weeks, down on the retail parks, the big supermarkets had already stopped asking people for their PINs and had gone back to printing out signature slips automatically.

Two months later the banks were confessing to journalists that implementation would be severely delayed by the costs they were asking the smaller shops to pay.

Shortly afterwards a letter from a shopkeeper appeared in *The Times* of London. He had received from his bank a plastic device to fit over the PIN pad, so that people couldn't see other customers entering their PINs quite so easily.

On eBay, the Internet auction site, a fingerprint recognition system was being sold in volume for only $25.

17

Too much Resolution?

*As Woodrow Wilson put it, 'If you want to
make enemies, try to change something.'
The story of BA and a strike at Heathrow*

In Britain the summer holidays begin when the schools break
up. This is usually around the end of July, and this is when
the holiday industry and all the associated services swing
into overdrive, prices rocketing as parents take their children
away for the school holiday period. Just as in France where
the autoroutes suddenly develop the sort of traffic jams that
cause environmentalists to have heart attacks, so the nation's
airports are no place for an agoraphobic. And busiest of all,
on one of the busiest weekends of the year, will be the hub of
British Airways operations, London's Heathrow airport.

Heathrow is the world's biggest international airport.
About 68,000 people are directly employed at the airport.
Of these are a sizeable number of British Airways front-line
and check-in staff, the vital link that convert people bearing
tickets into real passengers on BA flights.

BA has had a turbulent and sometimes troubled history
since the once state-owned British airline was privatised by
Margaret Thatcher in 1987 as part of the then Conservative
government's policy of divesting itself of non-core activities.
However, with passenger growth, new routes and the

buoyant economy for much of the latter quarter of the twentieth century it had grown and thrived, and at one time justly could claim the advertising slogan of 'The world's favourite airline'.

Things were not to remain rosy. The airline suffered from the downturn in the world economy during the early and mid 1990s, and a typical damaging strike of cabin crews in 1997 did nothing to improve its efficiency or reputation, costing BA some £125 million.

By the early 2000s, cost reduction and working efficiency was a priority for the management team at BA, and a large number of jobs had already been shed. In order to improve efficiency and defeat what they saw as working practices that short-changed the company by allowing workers to come late and leave early, BA determined to introduce electronic work timing with swipe cards throughout the organisation. This meant that they would know exactly when staff turned up and signed out, leading, it was hoped, to work improvements and lower costs. At Heathrow, some 2,000 of BA's staff had already accepted the new system.

But there was one group of employees who were not at all enthusiastic about the new swipe cards. These were the front-line staff. Predominantly women and frequently part-timers, these lowly paid employees had found in their BA check-in jobs viable employment that could be fitted around the complex modern demands of family and home. The introduction of electronic systems replacing the more human rostering they had come to rely on was seen as a threat. They had, through their union, been negotiating to allay these fears for a year. But the tectonic plates of the unions and the management were moving inexorably, and soon a clash was inevitable.

On Wednesday, 24 July 2003, the BA management decided that they would cease their policy of careful negotiation. They decided to adopt a 'one final push' solution. Staff arriving at work were presented with a fait accompli. The new systems had been, in effect, introduced overnight. The consequences were to be catastrophic.

Although the unions subsequently dissociated themselves from the wildcat strikes they must have been secretly delighted with the impact on the BA management team. Within days some 500 holiday and business flights (for BA carries many 'premium' passengers) had been cancelled. Around 100,000 passengers had been inconvenienced, made to wait, transferred to other airlines or sent away. The damage to BA's reputation was devastating.

Around the United Kingdom, the nation looked on slack-jawed. For although opinions were split as to the rights and wrongs of the action, the question hanging in the air was near universal, 'However did the BA management get into this mess?' The staff were front line, essential, and without them no passengers would fly. The staff had thought they were negotiating a difficult and, for many, job-critical proposal, for they held their working practices and flexibility very dear indeed. They had a strong union. BA had a history of difficulties with staff. The weekend was the busiest of the year. Anyone who had thought about possible scenarios would have realised the combination of risk and impact was unacceptable and chosen to act differently, or at the very least at a different time.

So what went wrong with BA's Recognition, Reality, Reconciliation and Resolution? It seems, with aftersight, that the BA management team had only seen the part of their current situation that they wanted to see, and consequently the Reality was false and the Reconciliation unwise. They knew they had a costs problem. They knew also they had some working practices that were possibly inefficient. They certainly knew they had strong unions. But it is possible that with their own security of salaried employment, their own professional and managerial working practices, their own ability to make things happen for them in family and work through influence and networks, that they simply did not recognise the importance of their existing rostering flexibility to many low-paid staff struggling to keep family and job intact. There was a work function and a social function in their staff's lives. The social equation broke down when the organisation imposed work changes, and the breaking of these social securities was the cause of the workplace strife with its appalling financial and reputational losses.

The final failing was again a failure of Resolution. For some reason the determination to drive in the changes swept all questions aside. It may have been a case of groupthink, the more cautious of the management not wishing to upset the group dynamics through overloud disagreement, or it may have been exasperation after a year of negotiating. Whatever caused it, the cumulative errors of Recognition, Reality and Reconciliation were magnified enormously by an excessively powerful Resolution.

The BA Secundi coefficient –
as an employee might have used it

Recognition. 'Have they not learned anything? Don't they ever come to the check-ins? Haven't they ever seen a holiday starting at Heathrow? Don't they realise how important those staff are? If they don't do the job, we can all go home! Recognition – I'd give them about 3, and that's generous!'

Reality: 'Well, they seemed to think that there was widespread fiddling going on, and that they needed to stop it. I don't think anyone likes to be regarded as cheating on the company. These people are allowed to have some pride without such suggestions being made. It's not as if they are a threat to the company, it wasn't urgent, it wasn't even very important. They should have just kept talking, that's what I'd have done. Reality? I'd give them, oh, say 5.'

Reconciliation: 'Well, if they couldn't see the truth of the matter, and they thought everyone agreed with what they wanted to achieve, they weren't going to get the solution right, were they? Completely wrong, going in like that to force their ideas through. Quite wrong. Give them 2.'

Resolution: 'Oh, typical Macho Management style, wasn't it?'

The Secundi coefficient for the introduction of swipe cards to check-in operators at Heathrow was therefore 0.33. Failure was twice as likely as success. There had been time to stop and think again.

18

Consider the obvious

The worst moment for an old joke: how the question to ask is 'What does this mean?'

It hadn't been an accident. She had known precisely what she was doing. In fact, ever since she had first heard the line or seen the cartoon, she had probably been looking forward to an opportunity to use the line. She had maybe read the story of the exchange between Oscar Wilde and James Whistler (Wilde, on hearing a clever remark by Whistler: 'I wish I had said that.' Whistler: 'You will, Oscar, you will'). Maybe like many other people she had taken to writing clever lines down for future use.

So here was the chance, and the ideal set-up. It even looked like the cartoon setting, in the airline boarding line, with the officer checking the bags, Horrifyingly, unhesitatingly, like a cliff-top collapsing in that horrible slow motion of the TV documentary programme, as her bag was taken for checking, quite intentionally and in full possession of her senses, she remarked, 'Hey be careful, I have three bombs in there.'

She wasn't a stupid girl. Well educated, literate, speaking five languages, confident in her spoken English, she had walked into a totally stupid mistake with her eyes open. It cost her the better part of a week in a US jail.

She later said that she had been at university in Poland when '9/11' had happened, busily dealing with her academic and health problems. She had not really been watching the world's media enough to appreciate the atmosphere that had developed. She just didn't know where she was, and why it was never again going to be a good joke. It was a joke from a suddenly, decidedly distant era.

But surely it was still strange. Walking into that airport, she must have been aware of the huge security presence. Aware also that the people in uniform were not laughing and smiling. Possibly hearing that the others in the line were being very serious about the checks and inspections.

Perhaps the most likely explanation was that she saw but did not recognise. We all fail in this some of the time. All around us things are changing, but we are busily doing other things, and so we notice but do not recognise. As individuals perhaps the consequences are minor; few of us would end up in a US jail as a result, like the unfortunate traveller here. But for organisations, the consequences of failing to recognise can be great. Organisations employ people, and through their wages enable them to live, own their homes, drive new cars and pay their taxes. The organisation is the bedrock of our society – if it fails to recognise what is changing, individuals suffer. When government fails to recognise great changes in the world, nations suffer.

19

Parallels and scenarios

'I left my heart in Santiago' – the vision of a global health market?

As a cliché, 'the world is changing' rates as one of the oldest and most fatuous. The fact that the world is changing is not the issue, the issue is what we are going to do in response. For the global changes, the macro trends, will have a direct impact on our organisations and the individuals who work in them. It is no longer possible to imagine that what is happening 'there' will not affect us 'here'. It will be for our change leaders to see what is happening, wherever it is happening, determine the change that needs to be managed and set the path for Reconciliation.

The ongoing, accelerating 'IT revolution' teaches us some lessons, and shows the importance of recognising even the first indications of major change. The pace of technological change in the latter years of the twentieth century and in the early years of the twenty-first was truly remarkable. It impacted directly or indirectly on nearly everyone in the western world, and the consequences are still filtering down to the developing world today. The Internet, to take one example, had the potential to create a shared, global future, with some companies using it to relocate jobs and make massive wage savings. But the Internet could also produce a divided future. The information held on the World Wide Web is mainly available to the generally computer-affluent West. This has the potential to create a knowledge 'closed circuit', which increasingly feeds on its own common information capabilities and tends to exclude less capable participants, which can mean entire countries.

A similar reversal can be seen in the changing shape of manufacturing. Industrial revolution after industrial revolution, technological revolution after technological revolution, have trained us to think that the competition for manufacturing jobs is constant and global. The world spent a decade or more reciting mantras such as 'the competitor is not in the next town, it is on the other side of the world'. The West has seen entire technology-based and manufacturing industries exported to low-wage economies. In the latter years of the twentieth century many developing countries were able to capitalise on their lower labour costs and participate in the global economy through the manufacture and assembly of goods for the global consumer market. This brought them employment, wealth and, for many, a step change in their economies and capabilities. As one country acquired the rewards of this work, together with the growth of their economies, their own labour costs grew, and western companies responded by transferring their overseas plants to 'new' low-cost countries.

Today, however, through constant integration and almost total automation, the labour component of many manufactured goods has become almost insignificant, even in the West, and that late twentieth-century labour cost advantage is gradually being lost. The countries which would have been the next generation, manufacturing and assembling manufactured goods for the first world, may not even be asked to participate. How will they respond?

One scenario is that they may respond, as before, by again taking the work that is too expensive in the West. One potential global shift, similar to that of manufacturing in earlier decades, may be the problems created for western countries by their longer lifespans. People may live longer, and be generally healthier and wealthier, but older bodies, like older cars, require more repairs. Already by the turn of the century early tales were emerging of British patients, unable to tolerate the waiting lists for hip replacements in their own National Health Service, going to France for their operations.

Suddenly the UK private health market became alarmed. For years there had been a thriving but very expensive private health sector, living on the premiums and payments from wealthier patients who were not prepared to put up with the waiting lists in the National Health Service. Almost overnight private health care companies like BUPA and Nuffield Hospitals found their competition might not be the 'free' but slow National Health Service for much longer. Instead, it could be very sophisticated private clinics half way around the world. A clinic, even a very capable one, is far easier to set up than a manufacturing plant, and many overseas countries have plentiful supplies of trained nurses, doctors and surgeons – the UK has been relying on them for decades to prop up its own hospitals. And all this time, successive governments have got UK patients used to paying for what was once thought free – with eye tests, dental treatment charges, costs for a range of ancillary treatments and drugs, all adding to a culture that has built up of 'going private' to escape waiting lists.

Were this global shift of medical treatment to emerge, the consequences would seriously affect nearly everyone in the United Kingdom. Firstly because the British National Health Service is Europe's largest employer, and the world's third largest, with over a million employees. That is equivalent to the population of Liverpool and Manchester combined. It has a budget of £40 billion, greater than the combined turnover of British Airways, Marks & Spencer and BT. The NHS budget represents about 5.9 per cent of Britain's Gross Domestic Product. The NHS treats 5 million patients a year. To do this it has to have a highly professional and educated workforce, so it is the second biggest purchaser of higher education in the UK. In short, the British NHS impacts on almost every citizen in the UK, even those it does not treat in any year.

British governments, the ultimate owners of the NHS, have been struggling for decades to reform the system. There have been constant efforts over the years to better use the resources, to cooperate or compete with the private health sector. Sections of NHS work have been partly privatised and large numbers of 'targets' imposed. All of these changes have been aimed at improving the service, and also at facing up to the inevitability of the UK's demographics, the changing age profile of Britain. By 2008 there will be 11.4 million children and 11.5 million older people, both of which categories are the heaviest users of health services. Advances in science and technology, including advances in biomedical research, will result in new forms of diagnosis and treatment, generating increased demand.

But what if the world of British healthcare is about to be rocked by major, radical change? What if the impact of global healthcare were to be as dramatic in its effects as was the rise of the low-cost manufacturing economies in the last decade of the twentieth century? In 2004, a survey by the polling organisation Populus, reported in Britain's *Sunday Times*, suggested that 66 per cent of British pensioners, the generation most supportive of the National Health Service, would be prepared to seek healthcare abroad. One company offering complete surgery packages for UK residents at its 22 Indian hospitals described the levels of enquiry in its first six months trading as 'immense'. Another said the market for overseas operations was 'explosive', driven by low air fares and a cost of operations overseas that are now within scope of an average credit card spending limit.

It is clearly time for the NHS to carry out a Secundi coefficient exercise.

Location, location!

Noon at Greenwich – the story of an improbable suggestion for timekeeping, and how small errors can become compounded

Today, as aircraft cross and recross the world on autopilot and supertankers with crews of only five cross oceans, it is easy to forget that behind these journeys lies an understanding of navigation that is built on centuries of science and discovery.

In the Middle Ages, tragedies at sea were the motorway mayhem of their time. Ignorance of position killed thousands of sailors a year, with ships coming to grief on reefs and rocks. In 1707, near the Scilly Isles off the southwest of England, four British warships ran aground with the loss of two thousand men. On long voyages captains and crew could find themselves sailing in circles for weeks, searching for their landfall. This in turn caused illness, as water ran low and food dwindled, and scurvy worsened and claimed lives unnecessarily. Only the best known, most used routes were sure of landfalls, and this concentration of traffic itself caused conflicts and accidents.

Navigators knew that to determine a position at sea it was necessary to compare the 'time aboard ship' with the time at their home port, at the same moment. They could then convert the time difference into a geographical value: since the Earth takes 24 hours to make one full revolution of 360 degrees, in one hour it completes 15 degrees. So each hour's time difference between the ship and its starting point means it has travelled fifteen degrees of longitude to the east or west of its home port.

Unfortunately, although navigators could figure out their local time at sea by watching the sun every day to see when it reached its highest point in the sky at noon, they could not keep track of the time at their home port. The pendulum clocks of the time could not be relied on as the ships rolled and skewed, and what pocket watches there were were hopelessly inadequate for navigation. A one minute error in the clock would signify one-third of a mile error in the course – more than enough to send a ship onto the rocks, or cumulatively to miss an entire continent at the end of a long voyage.

Schemes, devices and plans to solve the situation abounded, of which the craziest was the one based on what was called the 'powder of sympathy'. The method was based on a powder that when applied to a wound supposedly would cause pain in the wounded person, who would cry out or jump. Amazingly, the author claimed that if the powder was applied not to the wound itself but to a bandage that had previously been on the wound, the result was the same. The proposal was that each ship from Greenwich (the port of London) carry a wounded dog, leaving a bandage from the wound behind. At precisely noon each day the bandage would be dipped into a solution of the powder. The dog, wherever in the world it was at that moment, would yelp with pain, and the navigator mariner could then note the local time and so find his longitudinal position.

There are no records of the success of the method.

21

Expect no warning

*A short look at an historic prawn sandwich:
how the present is never secure*

One of the barriers to change is the fear that moving forward is more dangerous than staying put. Like bugs, we are skewered on the pin of uncertainty. 'If only we could be a bit more certain we were doing the right thing' is the refrain, and from this springs a reluctance to move too far from the apparent security of the status quo.

But this is an illusion. A study of the financial advertisements in any newspaper will reveal a dozen variations on the theme of 'past performance is not an indication of future performance' as a warning to the investor. History is littered with examples, usually of great crashes following spectacular rises.

Investors in Ratners, an established chain of high-street jewellers in the United Kingdom, would have had every reason to be confident in their shareholdings. The company was a fixture on British high streets, it was expanding abroad, profits were solid as a rock. Its chairman, Gerald Ratner, was a masterful business pilot, and the future looked both secure and bright.

Then one night in 1991 the chairman, in a speech to the Institute of Directors, joked that one of his firm's products was 'total crap', and boasted that some of its earrings were 'cheaper than a prawn sandwich'. The remarks were instantly seized upon by the media and an estimated £500m was wiped from the value of the company in weeks. Mr Ratner left the firm that carried his name the following year, and his name was expunged from the company in 1994.

So the idea that the present is a safer position is an illusion, and the real problem most organisations face is that of ensuring secure change.

No planned change is ever truly secure. A step in the direction of security can, however, be made by ensuring that the factors which will create the best chances of success are firmly in place. We can estimate from these the likelihood of success in the changes we plan. To some extent, we can also estimate the impact of changes we didn't plan.

22

Putting Secundi into practice

What do I do on Monday? Using the Secundi coefficient for individuals and organisations

By definition all organisational change involves a starting point and an end point. The starting point is where the organisation is at the outset, although it may not be where they would choose to start. Change involves a movement from that position. Movement may not take us to the end point the organisation desires, but it will at least not leave the organisation vulnerable.

Making no movement does not stop change, it simply reduces the chances of successfully emerging from it. The rabbit is said to be 'trapped' in the headlights, and its stillness does not save it. A 'sitting target' is not safer for its stillness. While Sleeping Beauty slept, the forest still grew. Such stillness is not to be confused with stasis, the state where opposing forces are balanced. When organisations do nothing, it is seldom stasis. It is usually a failure through unwillingness to move and to respond to changes that are going on around them, a position of danger, not security.

To choose to move, to determine where, how far and with what end goal requires a view of where the organisation is starting from. The problem, of course, is that most organisations are not sure where they are starting from. They think they know, they may have convinced themselves they know, but usually they are wrong. It is in fact rather like the fable of the blind men and the elephant,[1] with each department or division, each level of seniority, each employee having a different perspective and a different interpretation of what they see.

In order to make a first step towards successful change, it is essential all these different points of view are brought together and inspected. Some views will undoubtedly turn out to be mistaken, however obvious they seem. Some will turn out to be vastly more significant than they at first appear. Some facets will emerge almost by accident, some will forever stay hidden.

There are many ways organisations can gain a clear view of where they are, or 'reach Recognition', from surveys to consultation days, from customer appraisals to the most sophisticated consultancy tools. Whatever tools are used, the objective is to reach a point of Recognition in order to identify the starting point for successful change as accurately as possible.

Using the tools of understanding, the 'four Rs' of Recognition, Reality, Reconciliation and Resolution provide a practical and easy way of monitoring and directing change in the organisation, or getting to grips with issues in life. Two methods are suggested here, one for an organisation and one for an individual. These are far from being prescriptive but serve to introduce the 'Secundi' methodology. The 'four Rs', the key components of a Secundi strategy for change, have already been explored in the book.

> The Secundi coefficient:
>
> $$\frac{\text{Recognition} + \text{Reality} + \text{Reconciliation}}{\text{Resolution}}$$
>
> where the Reconciliation, Reality and Reconciliation are each values out of a maximum of 10, and Resolution is 30.

An organisational mechanism

1. Commence two essential information-gathering activities. The first is 'Recognition' (R1). Through telephone, e-mail, surveys, focus groups, brainstorming, records and conversations, find out where exactly your organisation is. What is right about it, and what is wrong? Gather information from colleagues, employees and customers, past and present. Get the true picture. As Cromwell said, paint the picture 'warts and all'. Record this on one side of a page of A4.

2. Move on to investigate the 'Reality' (R2). This is not 'the best we can do considering where we are', so you do not need to have the results of the 'Recognition' survey before you start. Start today. Find out what your competitors are doing or about to do. Find out what you will have to do but maybe have been putting off. Find out what other people think you need to do. Find out what will happen if you don't do anything. Record this on one side of a page of A4.

3. Take the results of R1 and R2 back to the people who gave you the information and get them to agree a score of 1 to 10 for the accuracy of the picture of your organisation that they portray.

4. Together with an implementation team drawn from the stakeholders you have already consulted, determine how to get from Recognition, where you are, to Reality, where you need to be. Write down, not using more than one side of a page, how you are going to do this. Together, award yourself up to 10 points for the accuracy of R3, your view of the Reconciliation you need. Add the scores for R1, R2 and R3.

5. One week after completing step 4 above, meet again. If everyone still believes the score they calculated at step 4, calculate the coefficient by dividing it by 30. Otherwise review the top line until you agree the values are right.

6. If your Secundi coefficient is between 0 and 0.5, you have major problems in facing up to the change you need to undertake. In all probability the data for R1 and R2 are inaccurate, possibly clouded by dogma or rationalisation, so the scores you awarded are wrong. You need to revisit these.

7. If your Secundi coefficient is between 0.5 and 0.7, you have only a slightly better than even chance of succeeding. Review R3 and R4 to ensure that R3 will deliver what you require and R4 will not be defeated by a failure of support or resources.

8. If you have a Secundi coefficient over 0.7, success is twice as likely as failure, but not assured. You need to ensure that your R4 score remains at a full 30 throughout the life of the process, and this requires continuing communication and constant review of progress towards R3.

A personal mechanism

1. Select an issue you are facing in your life. On one or more sheets of paper, write down everyone who is involved in this. Then write down, in one sentence each, what you believe they think of your current position.

2. Reflect on these sentences and decide how clearly these really describe your current situation. Award yourself a Recognition (R1) score up to 10. If it is below 7, decide how you are going to get better information on where you are and do it.

3. On another sheet of paper, write down using only as many sentences as you used for your Recognition score what you want your position to be when the issue is resolved. You can award yourself between 1 and 10 for how satisfied this would make you, but really you should score yourself at least 8.

4. Take some time to decide what changes are essential to move you from your current position to where you need to be. Write them down. Think about them. Make sure you have left nothing out, but also that each one is actually going to achieve a move

in the right direction. When you have these all to your satisfaction, award yourself between 7 and 10 points, depending how sure you are that you have it right. This is your Reconciliation score (R3).

5. Write down all the things that you will like about the changes you have to make. Write down all you might not like. Do not change the score you awarded for R1, R2 or R3. Be honest with yourself – who are you fooling but yourself?

6. Add R1, R2 and R3 and divide by 30. This is your personal Secundi coefficient.

7. If your Secundi coefficient is between 0 and 0.5, you have major problems in facing up to the change you need to undertake. In all probability you have been fooling yourself with your scores for R1 and R2. Take a day or two off, then do these again, perhaps being a bit more honest with yourself!

8. If your Secundi coefficient is between 0.5 and 0.7, you have only a slightly better than even chance of succeeding, but be sure everything in R3 is necessary, because some of it may have made your R4 score too high or too low.

9. If you have a Secundi coefficient over 0.7, success is twice as likely as failure but still not assured. Plan some quick successes from the R3 list to give yourself early rewards. This will help your Resolution up, so that you become more and more likely to succeed.

Note

1. The fable of the blind men and the elephant:

It was six men of Indostan
To learning much inclined,
Who went to see the Elephant
(Though all of them were blind),
That each by observation
Might satisfy his mind.

The First approached the Elephant,
And happening to fall
Against his broad and sturdy side,
At once began to bawl:
'God bless me! but the Elephant
Is very like a wall!'

The Second, feeling of the tusk
Cried, 'Ho! what have we here,
So very round and smooth and sharp?
To me 'tis mighty clear
This wonder of an Elephant
Is very like a spear!'

The Third approached the animal,
And happening to take
The squirming trunk within his hands,
Thus boldly up he spake:
'I see,' quoth he, 'the Elephant
Is very like a snake!'

The Fourth reached out an eager hand,
And felt about the knee:
'What most this wondrous beast is like
Is mighty plain,' quoth he;
''Tis clear enough the Elephant
Is very like a tree!'

The Fifth, who chanced to touch the ear,
Said: 'E'en the blindest man
Can tell what this resembles most;
Deny the fact who can,
This marvel of an Elephant
Is very like a fan!'

The Sixth no sooner had begun
About the beast to grope,
Than seizing on the swinging tail
That fell within his scope.
'I see,' quoth he, 'the Elephant
Is very like a rope!'

And so these men of Indostan
Disputed loud and long,
Each in his own opinion
Exceeding stiff and strong,
Though each was partly in the right,
And all were in the wrong!

John Godfrey Saxe (1816–87)

Tailpiece

In which we tell you why it
all seems so obvious

If this has all seemed a bit familiar, it's because it is. Or at least, like all the best models, the Secundi coefficient and its components are so obvious that they seem familiar. Over the years we have all grown used to the famous models we can use to look at our lives and our work, and they have become obvious. We can't believe someone would not accept them. We know that Joseph Luft and Harry Ingham's 'Johari window' is a simple representation of the truth of knowledge, even if when Mr Rumsfeld referred to it he was mocked. We know that most problems can, of course, be described using the fishbone or Ishikawa model of 'Men' (for it was pre-political correctness), 'Materials', 'Machines' and 'Methods'. The balanced scorecard is just, well, so sensible, isn't it? And team leadership can, of course, be described by the Adair action-centred leadership model of three interlocking circles.

When we have gone out to meet people, and we have explained to them the central proposition of the Secundi coefficient model, they have nearly always said, 'Well of course!' They then usually go on to tell us they have 'seen it somewhere'. The truth is that they haven't seen it anywhere, but it is so startlingly obvious that they feel they should have seen it.

This book has examined the model using lessons from many stories of individuals, organisations and societies. We hope that in several cases you will indeed have thought 'Of course!' or 'something just like that happened to me once!', and recognised in the episode a way of looking at your situation afresh. We hope that the thesis we propose, that there are four key success factors for leading change – Recognition, Reality, Reconciliation and Resolution – and that these are interrelated, has been made.

Finally, we hope you will find the Secundi coefficient a useful tool for looking at the challenges you face in life and work, and deciding where your strategy needs revision. But a word of caution: 'The future doesn't yet have any history for us to learn from.'

Bob Stott
George Edwards
2004